Dedication

From my heart, I dedicate this book to:

- My three beautiful children: Maxwell, Natasha and Asher
- Every man and woman who had a chance to live again after the 1994 Rwanda Genocide Against the Tutsis
- All our future generations, who are our children, our heritage and hope;
- My cousins, Adeline and Clarisse
- My adopted family of my uncle Rutabana Bernard
- My uncles Emile and J.M.Vianney; and all my extended family and friends

And to the memory of:

- My Grandpas and Grandmas, both paternal and maternal
- My Mama and Papa
- My brother César Uwineza (Kiki)
- My sister Solange Umugwaneza (Mimi)
- My brother Alestude Munyabugingo
- My baby brother Régis Dominique Shumbusho and baby sister Gatesi Bénédicte
- And late friends Claudette Umugwaneza and Martin Butarama

May your souls rest in peace.

Contents

	Acknowledgments	1
	Forward by Dave Brown	2
Chapter 1	The Home I Loved	3
Chapter 2	Shadows	16
Chapter 3	Born at the Wrong Time	30
Chapter 4	"Kill Them All"	44
Chapter 5	Waiting for Death	63
Chapter 6	"You Will Suffer But You Will Live"	77
Chapter 7	Facing Life Alone	91
Photographs		103
Chapter 8	Christ in Me	121
Chapter 9	A Reason to Live Again	133
Chapter 10	Too Evil to Forgive	144
Chapter 11	The Courage To Live Again	163
Chapter 12	Finding My Father's Body Remains	180
Chapter 13	A Lesson of Faith and Resilience	193
Chapter 14	Healing Through Relationships	204

Acknowledgments

- I wish to thank all those special friends who have walked such a hard journey with me to be able to make it where I am today. I thank God for each special friend that has come into my life especially for James and Tina Stacey.
- I wish to thank my extended family that has been there for me when I needed family and people to lean on.
- I wish to thank my family and the group of survivors that I have been part of to share our painful journey of healing.
- I wish a big thank you to Brad and Carol Mason and the Mason family for welcoming me to America and to my Successful Relationships Inc. family who has supported my children and me.
- I wish to thank my Pastors and church leaders at the Chapel family who have been a great blessing to my family and me.

Foreword

This is a true personal story of horrific cruelty and dehumanization in The 1994 Rwandan Genocide Against the Tutsis. It is also the true personal story of God's amazing grace in the life of a young woman who experienced both physical and spiritual salvation. But the author was not spared from exceptional personal trauma and "after-shocks" (PTSD) that have "pressed" her into deep dependence on Jesus Christ, the God she loves and serves. "Umuhoza", the author's name, given by family members, means "counselor/comforter" and readers will be "counseled and comforted" as she describes walking the path of forgiveness. They will be encouraged and instructed as she describes the desperate circumstances, the bold prayers and the extreme dependence on the Lord that have continued even to the present day. The story of this beautiful and gifted young mother graphically illustrates "the fellowship of His sufferings" (Philippians 3:10-11) and God's gracious suffering with His people—and His rescue of them (Isaiah 63:9).

Dave Brown, Pastor
Care and Connection Groups
The Chapel
4444 Galloway Road
Sandusky, Ohio 44870

Chapter 1

The Home I Loved

One of my treasured possessions is a little battered photograph of myself as a seven-year-old girl. Everything that belonged to my family was destroyed in the 1994 genocide that took place over a period of one hundred days in my country of Rwanda. The picture belonged to, and was given to me, by one of my uncles. It shows me standing in front of our banana plantation at home. I am wearing a simple white dress with blue flowers made for me by my mother. My hair is cropped short, as school rules demanded. I look quite serious, although I remember I was trying to force a smile. I was worried as to what was about to happen. I like the photo because it brings back so many memories.

First, my uncle is taking the photo and is urging me to smile. But I am more concerned about my mother who is standing just behind the camera. She is furious with me because the previous night – not for the first time or the last – I had stayed at my grandparents' house without telling her and I know that I will shortly have to face her. My mother, Primitive Bamurange, was a strict disciplinarian but she was also very loving. My father, Bernard Munyabitare, worked away from home, coming back mainly late at night or on weekends, so it was she who primarily created the homely family environment which made my early childhood so happy. The punishment came, as I knew it would, but then my misdemeanor was all forgotten and life resumed its normal pattern.

Second, I was a serious child. Probably overburdened with duties, but full of spark and with a zest for life. I was a bright and conscientious pupil at school – one of the best in my class, even though I was a year younger than the others – and the fastest runner. I grabbed all that life had to offer and, with parents who were keen for their children to have the best possible start in life, I had a great future ahead of me.

Third, and best of all, the family I loved. At this stage (in 1987), my family consisted of Mama and Papa, César (nine years old and nicknamed Kiki), me (seven years old), Alestude (four years old) and Régis (two years old), who was my favorite brother. Before Régis was born, I had longed for a baby to care for and had pestered my mother to provide me with one. As a result, when Régis was born, I lavished him with all my care and affection. I also had a sister Solange (nicknamed Mimi), who was César's twin, but she lived with my grandparents on the opposite side of the valley.

It seems that when I was born in 1980, Kiki and Mimi were very put out. They were afraid that this new baby would take their place in our parents' affections and wanted my parents to take me back to the hospital from which I had come. Their crying was so persistent and their jealousy so intense, that in the end my grandmother decided to take them to live with her, which was also a great help to my mother who was caring for three children under the age of two. When my brother Alestude was born, Kiki decided to return home as he now had a brother to play with, but Mimi remained with my grandparents. We saw her often as our homes were not too far apart, but it did mean that I was the only girl at home.

My mother and father were both hardworking and capable people, who provided us with a good standard of living. My father was a businessman and worked most of the time in Kigali, the capital of Rwanda, about fifty miles away. He ran a wholesale business supplying second-hand clothes to market traders, and as a sideline, he used his small car as a taxi. In addition to our traditional mud-brick home, which he gradually extended over the years, he also built three other houses – one in the Congo, one in our small town of Nyanza, and one in Kigali, which he rented out.

My father could be described as something of an entrepreneur. But his business acumen went hand in hand with a very generous heart. I remember many occasions when, on Sundays, knowing my father was home for the weekend, our neighbors would come and ask him for money that they needed to enable their children to receive hospital treatment or to go to school, or for any other problem they might have. Such generosity he had learnt from his own father.

My mother too was a very busy person. In addition to

looking after the home and plantation, which included cows, goats, sheep, chicken, ducks and turkeys, she tried her hand at various moneymaking enterprises, with help from a house boy and girl. One of these was a small shop, which she had set up in a room of our house with a door opening out onto the adjacent track. Here she sold the surplus vegetables from our plantation, such as cassava, cabbages, aubergines and avocados, as well as other basic household goods including salt, sugar, rice, soap and paraffin. She had also run a hairdressing business, which brought a steady stream of women to the house.

My mother's love of people and great trust in them meant that she often gave her services free of charge and for that reason she never made much money. But we had all we needed at home for my father worked hard to ensure his family was financially secure. "I'm working for you now," he used to say. "When you get older, you will work for yourselves." My father was not a very demonstrative man, but we children all knew that he loved us.

My parents were pillars of our local community. Through their hard work and enterprise they were perhaps better off than our neighbors, but their wealth was never a barrier because they were always so openhearted. Our neighbors worked in our plantation. When their son had a baby, my father lent him one of his cows so that the baby would always have milk. When the cow had a calf, my father allowed the man to keep it.

As well as my own home I also loved to be in the home of my godly grandparents, Stephan Munyabitare and Margaret Mukamajoro. When you stayed at their house, you could always guarantee you would go to bed late – and for no other reason than my grandfather's long prayers! It was an unwritten law that if you went to Stephen Munyabitare's house in the evening, before bedtime you prayed! The whole family joined in, as well as their workers and any visitors to the home. It could be very tiring for a little seven-year-old girl, but that never stopped me wanting to be there. I loved my grandfather. He was a man of great integrity who had tremendous love and care for all kinds of people.

Every time I went to Grandpa's house, there were always people waiting on the steps of his house for him to come out so that they could ask him for money. As a teacher, he was better off perhaps than many, but he gave because he had a heart to give. He was a good man, very kind and very loving. People would often ask him for his advice, particularly married couples that were having problems. Grandpa loved books, but above all he loved the Bible, which he was always reading. Sometimes in the evening people would gather together in front of his house so that he could teach them about the Word of God. He also served in his local Roman Catholic Church and led a weekly home group, which would read the Bible and pray.

Grandpa was always talking to us as his grandchildren about God. If we didn't go to church on any

Sunday, he would want to know why. He taught us never to lie and never to steal, and he explained all the Ten Commandments to us in a way we could really understand. He taught us both by word and by practice, as I discovered to my cost. I remember one day I took my friend's tennis ball without her knowing, because I wanted to play with it. Realizing I would get into severe trouble from my mother if I went home, I went to my grandparents' house – on this occasion, too, without asking her permission. I was having a lovely time playing with the ball when my grandfather came back from work and surprised me. I tried to hide the ball but he asked me, "What are you hiding?"

"Nothing," I lied.

"I know you're hiding something," he said, grabbing hold of me and discovering the ball in my pocket where I had tried to hide it. He wanted to know where I had got the ball, and I told him that my friend had lent it to me so that I could play with it.

"Does your mother know that you are here and that you have this ball?" he then demanded to know.

"Yes," I lied again.

Even though it was already late and not even putting his bags inside the house, he took me straight home. When he discovered that I had stolen the ball, he caned me himself and made me take it back to my friend that very night. I knew I had done wrong and I accepted my punishment.

By the age of seven I had already been attending

School for a year. Children did not normally start school until they were seven, but watching my elder brother go to school every day I was desperate to go too. When I was six, my father asked my grandfather to use his influence as a teacher to persuade the headmaster of the local school to allow me to do so. I was very happy and excited to start school, even though it was a wrench to leave my two younger brothers playing happily at home. It was an hour's walk to the Ecole Primaire de Nyakabuye, but my older brothers and I didn't mind, as there were lots of children from our village at the same school and we all walked together.

The noisy chain of chattering children in blue school dresses and blue shirts and khaki shorts hurried its way along the country tracks up and down the hills and through the woods, sometimes in the blistering heat and at other times in the torrential downpours of the rainy season. We knew we were the lucky ones – there were many children whose parents could not afford to send them to school. Our mother gave us strict instructions never to stop on the way to play and never to eat anything given to us by a stranger, because we had to go through an area, which was renowned for witchcraft and around that time several children had been poisoned.

In many ways starting school ended the carefree period of my childhood, since from the age of about six and a half my mother said that I was now sufficiently grown up to do a lot of work around the house. In term-time I would leave home early because each morning, of my own volition, I went to the six o'clock Mass at the Roman Catholic Church, where I was a server. Although the church was fairly near my school, I would still have to run hard to make sure I arrived by 7.30 a.m. when class started, as late children would be severely punished. This I did barefoot, since we weren't allowed to wear shoes so that poor children were not at a disadvantage.

When school finished at midday, we did the hour-walk back home, and then my brothers and I had to water the vegetables and flowers in my mother's gently sloping garden, which meant that we had to fetch water from the standpipe three miles away. If we could, we would save ourselves the walk by finding a small stream and draw the water from there. It was always a great relief when it was the rainy season. Then, while my brothers played, I had to face a pile of dishes, which awaited my return in the kitchen. And after that I had to settle down to my homework.

Harder to bear were my duties during the school holidays when, while my brothers played football or visited our cousins or their friends, I was required to do the housework. As the only girl living at home, it was my responsibility to do this, as our workers who normally did these jobs, were given a holiday.

"It's not fair," I would complain to my mother. "Why can't I go and play like César and Alestude?"

"You are the only girl here," she would say. "I want to

be certain that if anything happened to me, you would be able to take care of your brothers. And I certainly don't want you to grow up to be one of those silly girls who are good for nothing."

The thought that she might die really worried me and once I asked her, "Are you sick, Mama?"

"No," she replied, "but it happens to other people and it could easily happen to me."

I was shocked by her reply, and from that time I always prayed that God would never let me see the death of any of my family members but let me die before them.

So, while my brothers had fun, I would trudge the three arduous miles to the standpipe with a bucket of clothes on my head and a jerrycan in my hand. On the way back, as well as the clean clothes I would carry a jerrycan full of the water I needed to clean the house and cook dinner. The standpipe was in quite a remote place in the valley and I didn't like being alone there. People would talk about the snakes they had seen and I always felt on tenterhooks in case one should appear. Fortunately I only ever encountered dead ones. Some days my task was made a little lighter by the companionship of a neighbor's eight-year-old daughter who would come to do her family's washing. At least then we could chat as we worked and the place where we did the washing did not seem quite so scary. Also, the long walk back did not seem quite so lonely. If I did not complete all the jobs my mother had given me, she would give me a severe beating.

I hated staying at home while my brothers had all the fun. I hated being the only girl at home and wished that my sister Mimi could come back home and help me. She was so lucky to live with my grandparents and my father's twin sisters, Martha and Mary, who were in their twenties. I was so often jealous of the life of luxury that she lived and secretly thought that she was spoilt. So many times I wished I could be a boy because it was obvious to me at that time that boys were better than girls.

When it all got too much for me I would cry my heart out and plead and plead with my mother to let me have time to play. Sometimes she would put her hand on my arm and say, "It's not because I don't love you that I am treating you in this way. It's because I want to teach you how to do things properly." Occasionally she would give me one or two days to go and stay with my friends or my cousins. Often, so reluctant was I to return to my work at home that I pushed the visit a bit longer than she had said and then, when I did return home, she would really punish me once again.

Whenever I did have a chance to play, I preferred to play with boys rather than girls. I would play football with my brothers and ride on the bike we all shared. Of course, we would sometimes fight, as all children do, but there was a strong and loving bond between my brothers and me, especially with Régis. Régis was a very loving boy. He was mad on cows and wanted to be a herdsman when he grew up. We were always being co-opted into the role of cow so he could herd us around, and he would cry if we refused to play along. As the family joker Alestude was always making us laugh and was very popular among the boys at school. Physically, however, he was not very strong and he was often ill with malaria and other sicknesses.

With my father frequently away, my eldest brother César was very happy to step into his shoes, a role my mother encouraged. He loved being the "big man" and going off to market to do the shopping and he was always our protector at school. Each day he made sure that we all got home safely from school, particularly in the rainy season when the rivers were swollen and very dangerous. I, for my part, would enjoy mothering my brothers, making sure, for example, that they took their jumpers to school in case it should rain and hurrying them along to make sure we weren't late.

At the time I resented being the only girl and having to do so much of the work around the home, but looking back I can see that my mother's early training provided me with the skills I needed to survive in the days that lay ahead. I wish I could transport you back into that photo I have described for you and give you some idea of the beauty and tranquility of my remote home sheltering in the hillside. They call Rwanda the country of a thousand hills and as I looked out from my home, the gentle rolling hills stretched away in every direction. They were lush and green and provided the perfect setting for our rural farming community.

    Dotted across the hills, spread wide apart, were the small mud-brick homes of our neighbors, each with their pan-tiled roofs. Depending on the size of their land, each would have a small plantation growing the cassava, maize, bananas, beans and tomatoes they needed for food. For many, this was their only source of income and they were grateful for opportunities to work for people like my father and my grandfather with more land and earn a little cash to supplement their income, and that is why it was so hard for many of them to cover the extras that life threw at them at every turn. From our house you could see Felicità's tiny house in the valley to the right and, over to the left, much further up the slope, in a clump of three simple dwellings, was the home of Vitale, who was to play a huge part in my story.

    High up at the top of the opposite side of the valley to my house, was my grandfather's house. To get to it, we walked down past the huge avocado tree (by which I am standing in the photo), past my mother's extensive banana plantation, past the cassava plants and the sweet potatoes, then past the area where my mother grew her tomatoes, aubergines and cabbages – and my father had dug out a sizeable dam to raise fish for food – over the small stream in the valley and began the slow, tortuous climb up the other side. We hated that climb and as children we would stand in a long line, pushing each other up, but it was worth it when you got there because there was always a warm welcome waiting for you and invariably a plate of home-cooked food. Grandma's food always seemed to taste so much better than the food at home – much to my mother's annoyance.

There was no fear in the Rwanda of those days of my childhood. The community was at one. Our neighbors were our friends. The hills rang with the sound of my brothers' voices – in the hills sound carries for miles – as they played football on the meadow in the valley a short walk away, or swam in my father's dam. Making a living was not easy, but the community worked together for the good of everyone. That was the home I loved, but which is now lost to me forever.

Chapter 2
Shadows

"Good morning, Mr. Headmaster," the class chanted, rising to their feet as Mr. Morris came into the room. He was very strict at the best of times and classes would fall silent at the mere sight of him. Today his expression was even more severe than usual and I noticed his bald head was glistening with sweat. He immediately instructed the class, "Hutus, stand up."

About two-thirds of the children stood up confidently, looking around at their classmates who remained seated. As young as they were, they sensed the strength of their position. Mr. Morris counted the children standing and, motioning for them to sit down, then ordered, "Tutsis, stand."

I had made up my mind that I would stand when my three best friends, Claudette, Sophie and Honorette stood up, but when Honorette had stood up as a Hutu, Claudette had motioned to me not to stand, leaving me feeling confused. I was not really sure which tribe I belonged to, but I knew I must be the same as Claudette, because she was my best friend. I hesitated. Seeing Claudette stand as a Tutsi, I decided to stand too. Just at that moment the headmaster barked, "Come on. Be quick about it. I don't need any of your silly behavior." This caused the Hutu children who had stood moments before to laugh at us and left me feeling very cheap. My legs were trembling. Finally the headmaster told the children who belonged to Rwanda's third tribe, the Batwa, a tiny minority of the population, to stand and a couple of children did so.

The headmaster made a round of all the classes in the school asking the same questions and after school, as we made our way home, the talk was all about who had stood with whom. We now knew something our parents had never told us: we knew who was a Hutu and who was a Tutsi. The reason, I discovered, why Claudette knew she was a Tutsi whereas I didn't, was because her father often spoke about the fact that he had almost been killed as a boy during a period of great trouble for the Tutsis after the Tutsi king, Rudahigwa, had died in 1959. Not only were Claudette and I best friends, but our mothers were best friends too. I hated what had happened that morning and wished that the headmaster had not come to our classroom. It changed things somehow and, although we all still played together very happily, there was a lurking feeling that we were not the same.

The head count of Hutus and Tutsis came to be a three-monthly occurrence, as the headmaster complied with the government's directive, and each time it happened it reinforced my feeling of dread. Each time the Hutu children would laugh at us and goad us, and neither the headmaster nor our teacher would make any attempt to shut them up. I hated the sound they made and the atmosphere it created so much that on one occasion I even attempted my own silent protest and remained sitting quietly in my seat while the Tutsis were being counted. Noticing that I had remained seated, my teacher said, "Stand up, you stupid girl," and I had no other choice but to stand and be counted with the other Tutsi children.

Being a Hutu or a Tutsi had never been an issue in our family. In fact, it was something that was never even talked about. One of my father's best friends and his business partner, Vincent Nzigiyimfura, was a Hutu, as were many of our neighbors. When my parents held a party in the village hall to celebrate a family occasion, such as each of their children receiving First Communion, it was a mixture of Hutu and Tutsi friends who came.

Many Hutu children came to our house to play, and we would play at theirs. My mother was a respected member of the community. Many young women who were getting married would ask her to be their matron, which in our custom was a kind of mentor and supporter in their married life. This she was pleased to do for Tutsi and Hutu alike. She also taught us to care for all our elderly neighbors by taking them meals and fruit when they were not well and helping them with any jobs they needed doing. Tribe had never been an issue, and I could not understand why it mattered. I wanted it all to go away.

But it did not go away. Bit by bit things were changing in Rwanda, and I was scared. My fear intensified a few months later when, one Tuesday evening while we were waiting for the weekly play which we always listened to as a family to come on the radio, we heard a disturbing news report. The date was 2 October 1990. The previous day Tutsi rebels led by Fred Rwigema had attacked Rwanda from their base in Uganda. The report claimed that the rebels were being supported by Tutsis from within the country and it warned that these people – these "cockroaches" or "snakes", as the newsreader called them – would be rooted out and punished. I thought they were talking about real cockroaches and real snakes invading the country and was terrified by the idea. Although they tried to play it down, we could see that our parents were clearly shaken by this news report. They did not want to explain the situation to us, and we were left feeling alarmed and frightened.

Later that evening, out of our parents' hearing, we children talked about what we had heard. My elder brother Kiki, who was now twelve and often talked with the other boys at school about the political situation, took the lead. "Don't you know," he said, "that in 1959 there was a war, as a result of which many Tutsis were forced to leave Rwanda, and live in other countries?"

I vaguely recalled something we had learnt in our history lessons.

"They are the ones who are now coming back into the country," he continued, "and there is going to be another war!"

He tried to sound as if he understood what was going on, but I'm sure he didn't. His words, however, fuelled my anxiety, and that night I could not sleep. In the morning, convinced that we were all going to be killed, I refused to go to school. Mama tried to make light of the situation and tried to reassure me that there wasn't going to be any war. She said the rebels they were talking about were not human beings but small animals with long ears, and there was nothing to worry about. But I could see that she was lying and in her face I could see that she was afraid too. My father added his own words of reassurance that nothing was going to happen and life would just go on as it always had. I wished I could believe them.

When we arrived at school, there were groups of children standing together, discussing the news. It's not just me that's worried, I thought to myself. The atmosphere was tense. Was it just a coincidence that it was the day for the headmaster to come into class and carry out his head count once again? Once again, as the Tutsi children stood, the Hutus shouted and jeered at us, and the headmaster made no attempt to make them be quiet. On this occasion, however, our teacher, who was a Hutu, brought them to order.

Later that day, when I got home, I asked my mother a stupid question. "Mama," I asked, "why did you choose to be Tutsi? Didn't you know it was a bad tribe?"

"We did not choose it, my child," she replied. "We were born Tutsi. Nobody chooses what tribe they want to be. God makes you the way He wants you, and you can't complain about it." Her voice was trembling, and I could see that she was on the verge of tears.

In the days that followed I came to understand that the Tutsis who had been forced to flee in the early 1960s following a prolonged period of violence against them, in which many thousands were massacred and thousands more were forced from their homes, had been asking the government for permission to return home. These exiled Tutsis numbered in their hundreds of thousands – probably in excess of 700,000 people. The government had refused, saying that the country was too small to accommodate such an influx.

The frustration of those forced to live in exile had grown over time until they declared that if they were not permitted to return in peace they would come in war. Tutsis living as refugees in the Congo, Burundi and Uganda banded together to form the Rwanda Patriotic Front (RPF), based in Uganda. As we had heard on that first alarming news report, the government was accusing Tutsis within the country, particularly businessmen and other wealthy Tutsis, of giving them support, thus enabling them to buy guns and other arms.

Towards the end of that same academic year we arrived home from school one day to find no one at home.

Although quite unusual, we were not particularly worried. The house was locked but we knew where Mama left the key and we let ourselves in. We were a bit surprised that she had not left a message as she normally did. A little while later one of our neighbors, Felicita, who used to work for Mama when she needed her in the plantation, came running over to ask if Mama or Papa were back yet. We replied that Mama wasn't back yet, but that Papa was in Kigali. She gave us some shocking news.

"Your father came back earlier today after you'd left for school, and then, not long afterwards, soldiers came to arrest him. They've taken him away."

"Where did the soldiers take him?" Kiki asked.

"I don't know," she replied. "That's where your mother has gone – to try and find out where your father's been taken and see if she can find someone to help her get him out."

"But what did Papa do?" I asked.

"I really don't know, Frida," she replied, adding, "Let's just wait and see what your mother is able to tell us when she comes back."

Mama didn't get back until late that evening. At about 9 o'clock there was a knock at the door and we all ran to open it. "Who is it?" we asked through the door, because she had always taught us never to open the door unless we knew the person who was there.

"It's me, my children," she said.

As soon as we heard her voice, we opened the door

and we fell over each other as we all tried to greet her at the same time. She looked very tired. With her were our two cousins Sebakara and Adam Laurgin, whom she had asked to walk with her through the field which was a short cut to our house. After thanking the brothers and telling them to go straight back home as it was late, Mama sat down and we brought her something to eat, thinking that she must be very hungry. Then, unable to wait a moment longer, we asked, "What's happened, Mama? Where's Papa?"

"Papa has been put in prison," she told us, "but don't worry, because he'll be back very soon."

"Why, Mama?" I asked. "It's because he's a Tutsi, isn't it?"

"No," she said. "They're accusing him of giving aid to the rebels, but I've asked Vincent Nzigiyimfura to help him and we'll prove that it's not true. He's OK, and I'm sure he'll be released very soon."

It was horrible to think of my father being in prison, accused of something I felt sure he had not done. For our mother's sake we stemmed the tide of questions which we were all longing to ask and for once we took ourselves off to bed.

It was in fact three more days before my father was released. My mother had begged his Hutu business partner Vincent to help him and I think a bribe was probably paid. It was, however, not the end of the matter and my father was subjected to ongoing intimidation and threats, and he knew he was being watched. He decided to work mainly in Nyanza and to go to Kigali only when it was really necessary. He also sold his car in an attempt to play down his wealth and success as a businessman. In any case, traveling around Rwanda was becoming more and more difficult, and in order to leave the district everyone had to apply for permission. It goes without saying that permission was granted far more readily to Hutus than it was to Tutsis.

The more we heard about what was going on, the more we realized that my father had got off lightly. Some people who were arrested never made it out of prison again, having been beaten to death. Others were subjected to a long, slow death by having paraffin poured into their ear, which gradually burned its way through their body. Of those who did emerge from prison, a great many were never the same again.

Not long after my father had been released I awoke late one evening disturbed by unusual noises. Since my father had extended the house, I had my own bedroom in the main house with my parents, and my brothers shared another small house next door. As I entered the living room, I was shocked to see my father stagger into the house and then collapse onto the floor. He had been badly beaten and was covered in blood. He had been riding his bicycle along the isolated country roads home from work when he had been attacked, beaten with sticks to within an inch of his life and then the top of his little finger on his right hand had been brutally cut off.

I was terrified, expecting his attackers to storm into the house at any moment. Mama desperately tried to persuade him to let her take him to hospital but Papa would not hear of it. Although hardly able to speak, he made her understand that his attackers, none of whom he had recognized, had warned him of even worse consequences if he told anyone about the attack and if they ever saw him on the road again at night. Mama bathed his wounds and bandaged them as best she could and in the morning she took him to the hospital. They said that he had had an accident on his bike on his way home from work.

Around the same time Papa's cousin Rurangwa Gracien suffered a similar attack and three of his fingers were cut off. They were the lucky ones – many people died in such attacks. These incidents were never reported. Whom could they report them to? After that Papa started coming home earlier. My mother warned us not to say a word at school about what had been happening.

A month or so later family life was rocked once again by the news that my mother's two brothers had also been arrested. One day, while my mother was visiting her friend, Donnah, a young man whom I didn't know very well, arrived with a message for her. Since he seemed very tense and troubled, I decided to run and fetch my mother straightaway. We arrived back home to find him waiting impatiently outside the house. In private he told her that Uncle Narcisse and

Uncle Emile had been arrested that morning, also accused of helping the rebels. The young man was in a hurry to get back as he also faced the risk of being arrested and needed to get to safety.

    Mama tried to hide the news from us but we could see that she was very upset and desperately worried about the two brothers she loved so much. That evening she went over to tell my grandparents about it, but there was nothing anyone could do except hope and pray. Much later we heard that after weeks and weeks in prison where they were tortured, the two men were released. They immediately decided to flee the country and go to Burundi. The younger brother stayed there, but the elder brother went to join the RPF on the borders of Uganda. My mother never saw them again.

    These were years of great tension for the people of Rwanda. Sometimes things would seem almost normal, and then we would hear of another person being imprisoned, another person being beaten up, another person disappearing. Even more devastating was news of large numbers of Tutsis being massacred. The first massacre had occurred in October 1990, and there were two more in 1991 and another two in 1992. Although we knew it was Hutus who were carrying out these attacks against our tribe, somehow we could not equate them with the people among whom we had lived so harmoniously for so long, alongside whom we sat in church, with whom we played on the playground. Although as a young girl there was no way I could appreciate the grave implications of the evil that was tightening its grip on our country, I lived every day with the fear that cast its shadow over our lives. I saw it in my parents' faces, I heard it in whispered conversations, and I sensed it in the adjustments we were having to make to our lives.

Our days at Nyakabuye School which had begun so happily ended abruptly and cruelly. The whole family had attended a requiem mass for my father's uncle's wife held early in the morning and my brother, my sister and I had run for all we were worth to try and make it to school on time, arriving just five minutes late. Breathless we explained our reason for being late, but no notice was taken by the woman teacher who was on late duty that morning. She was a Hutu. Together with some other children who had also been late, we were forced to walk on our knees along a long stony path all the way to our seat in our classrooms. Each time we fell over with the pain, the teacher beat us with a stick. After a while she dismissed some of the other children and allowed them to return to their classes. These children were Hutus.

As the stones pressed into our knees, the pain was excruciating, not to mention the humiliation and sense of unfairness we felt. At one point Kiki suggested that we should get up and go home, but Mimi said that our parents would just think we were being disobedient to the teachers and would punish us even more. "No, they wouldn't," Kiki said. "They know we were at the mass." Hearing them talking, the teacher intervened angrily. Once again Kiki tried to explain that there was a good reason why we were late for school that morning, but she just slapped him across the face and told him he was lying. "Well, you can choose," she continued. "If you don't want to walk on your knees, I will cane you instead." We could see the hatred in her eyes as she caned each of us in turn.

When we arrived home that lunchtime, we were all dejected and very, very sore. I burst into tears as we explained what had happened to Mama. Both our parents were very angry at the punishment we had received which was clearly excessive. Mama insisted that Papa needed to change our schools before the next school year. He agreed with her, but the words he spoke next made a deep and lasting impression on me. "We can change their school," he said, "but the problem is not going to go away." At that moment I understood that the harsh punishment we had received had not been about being late, but had been because we were Tutsis. I didn't say anything, but recognition dawned in my heart.

The next day Papa went into the school to talk to the headmaster. He was very angry and ready for a fight – even a physical one. Since the headmaster wasn't around, he had to make do with voicing his complaint to one of the teachers. When he was told that the punishment we had received was in line with the policy of the school, he declared there and then, "Right. I am taking my children out of this school. They will not be coming back here ever again." That was fine, as far as we were concerned.

Chapter 3
Born at the Wrong Time

The following school year Kiki, Mimi, Alestude and I started at Gatagara Primary School, which was the school my grandfather had taught at prior to his retirement earlier that year. Régis was already attending the nursery at the school as my Aunt Clemence was one of the teachers. Gatagara Primary School was a school for disabled children, but it did have a few able-bodied pupils. My grandfather used his influence with the headmaster, who was married to his niece, to get us a place at the school. We were very happy to be going there. Not only was it a very good school with a Tutsi headmaster, but it was much nearer home – only a twenty-minute walk away. Another bonus was that it did not have a school uniform, and I enjoyed being able to wear what I liked. And, of course, when the head count came round again, no shouting or name-calling was tolerated from the Hutu children!

I was sad to have left behind my good friends Claudette and Sophie – our other friend Honorette had died of malaria the previous year. It had been very hard to lose a friend we loved so much. In my new class I was lucky to have four cousins, Valérie, Yvette, Eric and Olivier. Eric and Olivier had changed schools at the same time as us to go to one nearer to their home. Our teacher Cécile was a Tutsi and there was an equal number of Hutus and Tutsis in the class. Cécile was an excellent teacher, treating everyone the same and only punishing children when it was really necessary.

It was an important year for Kiki and Mimi because it was their final year at primary school, in which they would have to prepare for their national examination. That year the school system nationally was due to change and the amount of years children spent in primary school was being reduced from eight to six. That meant that I, now aged twelve, should be taking the national examination at the same time as the twins. However, since I was already a year younger than my classmates, my parents felt that I was not ready to leave home to go to boarding school (which was the normal pattern for brighter students), and so at the new school they made me repeat Year 5. I wasn't at all happy to be put back a year with children who, although my age, seemed much younger than me, especially when I felt ready to take the exam, but I knew I had to respect my parents' decision. Being in a new school with good teachers made up for my initial disappointment.

Since our previous academic year had been so disrupted, Papa arranged for us all to have some private tutoring after school on Tuesdays and Thursdays, together with the cousins who were in my class. For this we went down to a school for blind children where our tutor taught. It didn't really help as Kiki and Mimi both failed the exam. Failing the exam was not particularly unusual, since there weren't enough public schools to accommodate all the bright pupils and the places did not always go to the most deserving. Many gifted Tutsi children were passed over in favor of less able Hutus. Both Kiki and Mimi went on to private secondary schools in Nyanza, Mimi choosing to study Commerce and Accounting at one school and Kiki Car Mechanics at another. Papa bought them bicycles to enable them to get to school, as it was much too far to walk. Since Mimi still lived with my grandparents, the twins would meet up along the road and ride together. Sometimes, if Papa wasn't particularly busy, they would meet him for lunch in Nyanza. Now that he was no longer able to go to Kigali, Papa's business was gradually going downhill. He tried to put a brave face on it, but at times I could tell that he was deeply troubled.

Each afternoon I would try and make sure that my two little brothers Alestude and Régis did their homework. I had no problems with Régis who was doing well at school, but Alestude found school work quite hard and was always trying to come up with a way to avoid doing it. Sometimes he would hide his homework or he would fall asleep when he was meant to be doing it. If I got angry with him, he would always cry and apologize, and then I would feel sorry and do it for him. His teachers could not understand why, when his homework was always so good, he would often fail his exams.

About this time I began to realize that Mama was

pregnant again. Nobody had said anything about it, but I could see that her body was changing and I put two and two together. I was very happy about the prospect of a new baby in the family. Without saying anything, I looked out the clothes that Régis had worn as a baby and washed them and hung them on the line.

"What are you going to do with those little clothes?" Mama asked, obviously surprised.

"We're going to have a baby, aren't we?" I replied.

"Who told you we're going to have a baby?" she wanted to know.

"Nobody," I said. "I just saw for myself."

"What a grown-up girl you have become!" she exclaimed. "You're right. We are going to have a baby. What would you like it to be – a boy or a girl?"

"A girl, of course!" I said without a moment's hesitation. "There are enough boys in this house." Then I added, "When she grows up, perhaps she can help me with the housework."

Mama smiled and said, "Well, let's wait and see. Whether it's a boy or a girl, God gives us what He wants, not what we want." A few months later Papa fell ill with a problem affecting the blood vessels in his feet and legs which caused them to swell. He was in terrible pain and had to remain in bed the whole time. By now Mama was heavily pregnant. It worried me to see her working so hard. She was obviously becoming more and more tired, and the strain of managing the house and plantation as well as taking care of Papa was taking its toll on her. Although it was near exam time I suggested that I could take a few days off school to help her, which would release the houseboy to undertake some of the heavier work in the plantation. To my surprise she agreed, and I was very glad to be able to make life a bit easier for her. This time I didn't complain about doing the cooking, cleaning, washing, and other chores because I knew I was helping Mama, Papa and the baby.

A week later, not long after the whole family had gone to bed at our normal time of 7 o'clock, something woke me up. I immediately became aware that Mama was struggling with her breathing and I went to see if she was all right. She looked terrible, and she was experiencing great difficulty trying to get out of bed. Papa was so ill that he could not help her in any way. Gasping for breath she told me to go and fetch her things from the cupboard. All women in our village would prepare themselves in case they went into labor in the middle of the night and could not get to hospital in time. I knew where Mama had put the things she would need for the labor and ran to get them. The thought of leaving her even for a minute terrified me. Looking back I think it was probably just normal labor pains, but at the time I was convinced she was going to die.

When I got back I found her trying to make her way to our outside washroom, which was a very small room with a concrete floor and no roof. Since she could hardly move I needed to help her. As soon as we reached the washroom she told me to run and wake Kiki and our houseboy Cyprien and tell them to fetch our grandmother, and then to heat up some water. This I did, but rather than Grandma I told the boys to fetch our neighbor Felicita. I was afraid that by the time they got to Grandma's house Mama might have died.

Then I lit the fire in the kitchen, which was no easy task, and put the water on to boil, all the while praying that God would save Mama and the baby. As soon as this was done, I ran back to Mama. At that very moment she let out an excruciating scream and I could see she was in terrible pain. I started to cry. I didn't know what to do. Five minutes later she screamed again and this time I heard a baby's cry. It was 12.25 a.m. I made as if to move nearer to her, but she told me to leave her until she had finished what she was doing. I didn't really understand what she meant but I did as she asked. As I left the washroom there was a loud knock at the door and I went to answer it. It was the boys returning with Felicita, who went straight to Mama. I heard another agonizing scream and I really thought she was going to die. Felicita shouted, "It's OK now. It's all over," and the baby cried again. I felt an immense joy wash over me.

Felicita called for me to bring the hot water. As I took it in, I caught a glimpse of the baby and I longed to hold it, but I could see it was not the right moment. "Is it a boy or a girl?" I whispered. In a very tired voice Mama replied, "It's a girl, just as you wanted, Frida." Returning to the other room where my brothers were waiting, I jumped for joy and told them that we had a sister. They smiled and relaxed, glad that it was all over.

As I went back into the main house, Papa called out to me, asking if the baby was born and whether it was a boy or a girl. "It's a girl, a beautiful girl," I told him, even though I hadn't actually seen her yet. I hovered outside the washroom in case they needed anything. After a little while, Felicita brought the baby out and handed her to me. She was now dressed and swaddled in a soft blanket. Calling to Kiki to bring the lamp, I took her quickly into the house so that she would not get cold. Once inside, the boys all gathered round to see her for the first time. As we uncovered her face which was buried in the blanket, we saw that she was absolutely beautiful.

Hearing our voices, Papa shouted to me to bring the baby to him. As he held her in his arms, he said to her, "You are a real surprise!" I think he was referring both to the fact that they had not expected to have another baby after Régis and that she had come so unexpectedly during the night, giving no sign the previous day that she was about to be born. His voice was very flat, and I could not understand why he was not rejoicing in the birth of his baby as we were.

For the rest of the night Mama and baby slept in my bed and I slept on a mattress by their side, so that I could help Mama with anything she needed. Before I fell asleep, I asked her, "Mama, do you think I could stay with you again today and not go to school for one more day?"

"No, Frida," she replied. "You've done enough, and you've got your national exam coming up. You should go to school. Grandma will come over and help me. But thank you for being so courageous tonight."

On the way to school that day I could not help but tell everyone I met that my Mama had had a baby, even if they didn't ask me. It was 18 March 1993. Four days earlier I had celebrated my thirteenth birthday and in five days' time Alestude would be ten. I liked the fact that we were all going to be having our birthday in the same month.

For several weeks after she was born my baby sister had no name. We just used to call her "Bébé." As time went on, Mama complained to Papa, "Why aren't you giving the baby a name?" Papa looked very sad and said, "I have no name for this baby." Then in our language of Kinyarwanda he spoke the word *Gatesi,* meaning "careless" or "reckless." By that he meant that she had been born at the wrong time.

"What kind of name is that for my child?" Mama said. "Can't you think of another name? Give her a good name."

"No, there is no other name that I can give her. She is Gatesi."

That same day, wanting my little sister to have a prettier name, I looked up the feast-day for the day she was born, which was the Feast of St Bénédicte. So she became Gatesi Bénédicte, but everyone called her by the name my father had given her: "Gatesi." In June that year I took my national examination and to my great excitement I passed it. I was given a place at a boarding school in Byimana which was a two-hour bus drive from home, with quite a long walk from our house to the bus stop. Since it was my father's old school, I had heard a lot about it, and it had been my dream to go there. The following September I left home with a mixture of sadness and anticipation.

My father took me to the school and helped me settle in. To his surprise he discovered that the school still had the same headmaster as when he was a boy – a stately old Belgian. I quickly made friends with a girl called Oda who was also new to the school. We were in the same dormitory, sharing it with ten other girls, and soon became very close. I also met another of my cousins, Karabo, although we didn't realize we were related until her parents came to visit her and made the connection.

In December we had our first holiday and I looked forward to seeing how my little baby sister had grown. When I had left home she was a strong and happy five-month-old baby. When the bus arrived in Nyanza, I was pleased to see Kiki waiting for me with his bike, because I had been wondering how I would manage to carry my bag home. I plied him with questions about how everyone was doing and he replied that everyone was fine. Whatever question I asked, he never seemed to mention Gatesi, and I found it odd. "Is Gatesi walking yet?" I asked. His answer was evasive, and he quickly changed the subject by asking about my journey and about how I was getting on at school. It reminded me of when Mama had come to see me at school in November. She too had seemed to skirt round all the questions I had asked about the baby.

When we arrived home, we found Mama sitting on a chair outside the house. She didn't look at all well. After we had greeted one another, I immediately asked where Gatesi was. "You'll see her. Don't worry," Mama replied. "Have a rest first." This was very unlike my mother who would normally have given me work to do the moment I walked in the house – now she was being nice to me and forcing me to rest!

While Mama was fetching me some food, I impatiently asked Alestude where the baby was. "Is she over at Grandma's?" I asked him.

"Mama will tell you later," he told me.

I knew something was wrong.

As soon as I woke up from my nap, I went to find Mama. She was in her room.

"What's happened to Gatesi?" I asked.

"I can't keep the truth from you any longer," she replied. "But I need you to be strong, as we have all had to be."

At that moment the horrible thought crossed my mind that Gatesi might be dead, but I quickly brushed it away. I couldn't believe that she could have even been sick without anyone telling me.

"What's happened, Mama?" I asked again.

"I don't know how to tell you this, Frida," Mama said, "but Gatesi is dead. She died in October, but be strong." The tears were running down her face and she could hardly finish her sentence.

I burst into tears and ran out of the room. How could they possibly not have told me that my little sister had died! How could they have buried her without me being there? Didn't I matter in this family? I felt very angry and very hurt. Shut out.

My mother followed me into my room. She was crying too. "I'm very sorry we didn't tell you, Frida. It was your first term in your secondary school and we didn't want to make it even more difficult for you. We knew you would be heartbroken. Forgive me. I'm very sorry. I know you really loved her, I just couldn't tell you."

"Why did you keep on lying to me when I got here?" I burst out.

"I didn't want to tell you the bad news as soon as you got here. You've been away a long time. There is no way I could tell you the moment you arrived."

I was devastated. Kiki took me to see Gatesi's grave and for days and days I cried and cried. It was two days before I was able to ask my mother what had caused Gatesi's death. She told me that they had taken her to hospital with malaria. Although she was ill her condition was not critical. Since as a baby the medicine could not be given in tablet form, they decided to put her on a drip. Her arms were still too small for the drip to be inserted, so it had to be put straight into her head. My parents believed that the Hutu doctor administering the injection into her head had deliberately twisted it so that she would die. Her condition deteriorated rapidly immediately after the drip had been inserted. In those days not many Tutsis who went into hospital came out alive.

  The days of that holiday passed by in a blur as I struggled to come to terms with the loss of my little sister. I had expected to spend all my free time playing with her in the garden and her absence left a huge hole. The tragedy of her death and the continuing tension in the country were taking their toll on my parents too. There was a great deal of unrest in Kigali, fueled by clashes between rival political parties which erupted into riots. There were increasing incidents of people being killed by bombs which had been planted in crowded places and hand grenades being thrown into taxi-buses or passing cars. Although my father no longer worked in Kigali, he did need to make occasional trips into the city to conduct his business. If my father was ever late home from work, Mama would become extremely agitated. Kiki and I would try to keep her company as she waited anxiously for him, but we often found it very hard to keep our eyes open.

  The trouble spread to Nyanza, and my mother was constantly warning us to be on the look-out for danger. She told us to be wary of the people we were sitting next to in the taxi buses and to be on the look-out for bags where bombs might be hidden. I was scared to death one day when I almost got caught up in a riot and, whenever I could, I preferred to stay within the refuge of our home.

My father tried to keep in touch with what was happening by listening to the radio. In secret he would listen to Radio Muhabura which was the station of the *Inkotanyi* (the RPF), but knowing how dangerous it would be if he were caught, having already been accused of being a collaborator, as a smokescreen he would also listen to Radio Télévision Libres des Milles Collines (RTLM), which had come on air during 1993. It was a propaganda machine which delivered a message of hate against the Tutsis and, as time went on, it saw less and less need to veil its aim of seeing the whole tribe exterminated.

We began to hear rumors that lists had been compiled of the Tutsis who were to be killed. I even heard that my old headmaster Mr. Morris from Nyakabuye School had been involved in drawing them up. When I arrived back at school after the Christmas holidays my Hutu classmates began to taunt me that I was on one of these lists and that it would not be long before I would be dead. "One day we are going to kill you," they kept saying. It was horrible. The Hutu girls in our dormitory also began to turn nasty and Oda and I asked for permission to move in with some older Tutsi girls we knew in another dormitory, but our request was refused.

Going back to the dormitory began to be quite an ordeal and there were many nights when I lay awake, terrified in case one of the girls put their menacing threats into action.

My worst fears were confirmed by an incident that happened at the school. We were all in the dining room one evening when there was a power cut. In the darkness the Hutu children started chanting, "Kill the Tutsis... Kill the Tutsis..." I was really scared and hid under one of the tables. When the lights came back on, it was discovered that a Tutsi boy called Eric had been stabbed with a knife during the blackout. The wound wasn't serious, but there was blood everywhere, and all the Tutsi children were very shaken.

Shortly afterwards my father came to see me and I told him what had happened. He comforted me by saying that it must have been an accident and that nothing was going to happen at school. His words went some way to reassuring me and after his visit I felt a bit calmer.

I was very glad when the term ended and it was time to go home for the Easter holidays. I was happy to be with my family again. I did not know that by the time I went back to that school my whole life would have been torn apart.

Chapter 4
"Kill Them All"

It was 7 April 1994 – a Thursday. I was soon to go back to school and my parents were planning to make a trip into Nyanza that morning to buy me all the things I would need. Listening to the radio as we usually did, we heard the news that would put an end to our family life forever. The news reader solemnly announced that the President of Rwanda, Juvenal Habyarimana, a Hutu, was dead. His plane had been shot down while preparing to land at Kigali airport the previous evening. The President of Burundi had died with him. The news had already been broadcast the night before but we had not heard it. The announcement concluded with the ominous instruction that everyone should remain where they were until further notice.

We children jumped up and down with joy. "Hurrah!" we shouted. "The President is dead. Now we'll get to go to the good schools! Now we'll have the opportunities we couldn't have before!"

"Be quiet!" my father snapped. "You don't know what you're talking about. This is the worst possible thing that could have happened. This is going to mean serious trouble for us – and I mean serious."

Of course, we were too young to understand what he meant, but later on, when we were on our own, Kiki said to me, "I understand what Papa meant. We are on the list and we are going to die."

"No, no, no, it's not possible," I protested. "It could only happen if they sent soldiers into the area. Our neighbors wouldn't kill us. There is no way that they would kill us. We're not going to die."

One of our parents' friends, Marie Rose, who was Mimi's godmother, was at our house. She had moved out of the district and had come back to pay us a visit. When the announcement came on the radio, she became very agitated. "I'm not staying here," she said, "I must get back to my husband and my children." She was married to a Hutu. Mama tried to stop her, fearing she might be killed on the way home but she grabbed her bag and left.

Shortly afterwards Papa went into Nyanza to find out what was happening. It was not long before he came back, looking very grave. "Things are very bad," he said. "There are roadblocks everywhere. All the arrangements are in place for the killing to begin." My parents had given up trying to pretend that everything was going to be OK. Later that day my father and some other Tutsi men had a meeting at which they agreed that they would defend their families if the Hutus came. They would not attack anyone, but they would not stand by while their families were murdered.

From that night on, fearing that our house might be burnt down while we were sleeping, we slept out in the forest close by. Mama told us to put on several layers of clothes – a couple of pairs of trousers and two or three jumpers on top. We would sleep in the middle of one of the huge bushes, all huddled together and very afraid. During the day we would return to the house for a very short time to get something to eat and then go back and hide. Papa and the other men armed themselves with clubs and machetes and roamed around the area, trying to protect their families.

Nothing happened to us that day, but the stories we heard of what was going on elsewhere convinced us that it would not be long. It was clear that the lists about which we had heard actually did exist. Within hours of the President's death, the people whose names were on the lists began to be visited and slaughtered in their homes, including moderate Hutus who would have been against the mass killing of Tutsis. Bands of trained killers known as the Interahamwe led the way, often dressed in flamboyant yellow, red and green, but all Hutus were forced to join in. Those who refused to comply were threatened with death.

People fleeing from Kigali began to stream through our area, each face betraying its own story of abject terror. They told of people fleeing into churches, schools and hospitals for safety, only to be surrounded by hundreds of killers who threw hand grenades into the building before entering and setting upon their helpless victims with machetes, clubs, spades and any other tool they could find. Death was often not these killers' sole aim; their aim was to inflict death as cruelly as possible and so it was preceded by beatings, torture and mutilation, and for many, many women by brutal rape.

We were the "enemy." It was not long before the RTLM was broadcasting the blatant message, "Kill the cockroaches! Kill the snakes! Find those Tutsis wherever they are and kill them. Kill them all, the old, the young, men and women. Don't even be afraid of killing pregnant women. We need to rid our country of this evil." There was a song they used to play on the radio:

> *Umwanzi wacu n'umwe*
> *Turamuzi*
> *n'umututsi.*
> Our enemy is one
> We know him
> It is the Tutsi.

With so many people coming to our area to try to escape, we began to wonder where we would go when our turn came. We were now in no doubt whatsoever that come it would.

A couple of days later Mama asked Papa to take the boys to the hairdresser's to get their hair cut. "I want them to look smart when they are killed," she said. She also packed some of our clothes in a suitcase and took them over to our neighbor Felecita's house, even though this old friend of the family had become increasingly hostile towards us. "Please could you keep these for me?" she asked. "If we survive, I will come back for them."

After a few days of sleeping in the woods, Régis was beginning to get very upset because he was so disturbed, frightened and overtired, and Mama decided to take him home in the hope that a decent night's sleep would help him cope better. She hadn't been home long when there was a great deal of shouting not far from the house and Mama's best friend Beatà, Claudette's mother, arrived at the house looking absolutely terrified. She told Mama that her husband had just been killed and her house had been set on fire, and pleaded with her to look after two of her boys, Bébé, who was five, and Olivier, who was four. She had taken her other five children somewhere safe but now she needed to go and find them. She went off, taking with her one-year-old son Lambert.

After that Mama knew that she couldn't stay at the house and came straight back to the forest with the three children. The little four-year-old boy, Olivier, was in deep shock. He couldn't speak; he couldn't even cry. He didn't seem to understand what people were saying when they spoke to him. He wanted to be on my mother's back the whole time. We wondered if he had witnessed his father being murdered.

Mama had not been back long when Papa arrived, running. Never before had I seen him look the way he did. Quickly explaining that soldiers had arrived with guns and that, when they had started to shoot, everyone had scattered, he told us, "The only thing we can do is make a run for it." When I heard him say those words, I knew that we were not going to survive. Papa said to Mama, "Try to take the children to some of our neighbors. We haven't been bad neighbors. Perhaps they will hide them for a few days until we see what's going to happen." Then he shouted to the group of about thirty other people who were with us in the forest, "Run for your lives. They're coming. Just get out of here." Everyone started running in different directions. My mum, my brothers, my sister, the two boys and I started running towards the school for disabled children, but a Tutsi who came running from that direction shouted at us that they were already killing down there and burning houses. People were running here, there and everywhere, and we just didn't know what to do, so we ended up going back into the forest. All around us everyone was talking about the people they knew who had been killed.

Mama told my sister Mimi, my cousin Valérie, who had also been sleeping in the forest, and me to go to the house of one of our Hutu neighbors, Esily, and hide there, saying that she would come for us in the morning. "But Mama, he won't let us," I said. "If he doesn't," she said, "just run for your lives."

It was just beginning to get dark when we arrived at Esily's house. Normally a friendly and approachable man he glared at us with his hands on his hips and demanded, "What are you doing here?"

"Mama told us to come here," we said. "Things are terrible."

"I know things are terrible, but what have you come here for?"

"Mama asked if you would let us sleep here for tonight, and she will come and get us in the morning."

He laughed, probably thinking that she would not see another morning. "You can't sleep here," he said.

"Please," we pleaded, "just tonight. We'll go in the morning."

His wife intervened. "Just let them stay tonight. They can go tomorrow."

Even though one of their children had been in the same class as me at primary school, they did not let us sleep in the same room as their children, but they just got out a grass mat and laid it out on the floor, near the door. "You can sleep there," they said. They did not even give us a blanket, just another grass mat to cover ourselves with. We were freezing. We all three lay there, but I don't think any of us slept. Everything was going round and round in my head. What was happening to Mama and the boys? How was she going to manage to run with that little four-year-old boy? What had happened to Papa and my brothers? Were they safe somewhere? How could people change like that? And I thought about what it would be like to be killed with a machete. The night was very, very long – much too long. We did not dare to speak to one another; we just lay there, tormented by our thoughts.

The next day was a Saturday and Esily and his family were Seventh Day Adventists. Esily's wife and children went to church – they had nothing to worry about because they were Hutus. Esily went out too, but we were not sure if he also went to church. They had not given us anything to eat or drink, and neither did they seem to care and we were very hungry and thirsty.

Around mid-morning Esily arrived back. We could see he had been running. "You have to go now," he said.

"Please let us stay," we begged. "Where can we go?"

"No, you must go. They may come and search the house, and I don't want you to die here. You have to leave now."

We pleaded and pleaded with him to let us stay, saying that we did not know where our parents were or where we could go, but he was adamant. As we were leaving he said, "All the Tutsis are up on the mountain, so that they can see the killers coming. Go and join them."

We ran as quickly as we could to the small mountain covered with boulders behind the village which was known as Ruganzu Rocks. Many Tutsis from my village and surrounding villages had gathered there. In the crowd I saw my mum's friend who was nine-months' pregnant who in the end had her baby not long after then, was raped and baby killed in such a horrific way yet she herself survived and has to live with these memories. Not only did she lose her baby but her husband and her other three children. Some of the young men among us were holding machetes and stones but you could tell from the look on their faces that they weren't going to be able to use them. All hope had drained away from these people and they knew they were going to die. I found my three brothers but neither Mama nor Papa was there.

"Have you seen Mama?" I asked Régis.

"No, I don't know where she is. We got separated. Perhaps she's been killed."

I do not think at nine years old Regis had understood fully what this meant. Even though you could tell that he was scared, part of me still thinks at the beginning kids thought it was funny that we were all running all day not understanding that this was a matter of life and death. It was no joke after they saw their family friends cutting them or their family members with machetes that they understood the terror and hate within those Hutus' hearts.

People did not seem to realize that although they had fled to the mountain so they could see the killers coming, they were also making it easier for the killers to find them. Children were crying; the elderly were stunned into silence, knowing that when the time came they would be too weak to run. I tried to keep hold of Régis' hand, but he kept tearing it away from me.

A little while later Régis screamed, "The killers are coming. The killers are coming." He had seen the sunshine glinting on the brand-new machetes the government had supplied them with. There were hundreds of them. As they marched towards us they were singing their disgusting song, "Kill, Kill them all. Kill the babies, kill the mothers, kill the young ones, kill the old ones..." In front of the killers marched a line of government soldiers carrying guns, who had been sent into the area to mobilize the local Hutus. They were ready to deal with any Tutsis brave enough to put up any resistance and that was the only time a Tutsi in my village could be offered a bullet without paying for it.

Suddenly shots were fired as a sign for the Hutus to start their job of killing, and panic erupted. There was a stampede as people started running in all directions. We joined a group of people fleeing towards another mountain where they hoped to be able to hide in the forest. As we approached it we saw that the way was impeded by soldiers firing into the air to scare people, so we all turned round and ran back the way we had come. In the confusion I lost sight of my brothers and my sister. After a while I came across my grandmother and my two aunts, Martha and Mary. They were carrying my two little cousins, Claire (4) and Uwera (5), who had been staying with them for the school holidays and got to find my sister again.

We ran and ran. We were trying to get to the primary school where we thought we might be able to shelter, but as we made our way down the valley towards the school we saw a group of killers slaughtering people with their machetes. We changed direction and tried the headmaster's house, but it was locked and everyone had left. We were all exhausted. Then my grandmother made a decision. "We'll go home," she said, "and we'll die there."

"We can't go home, Grandma," I said. "We'll be killed if we go home."

"We'll be killed wherever we go," she replied. "It's happening all over the country. Nowhere is safe. We'll have to go home."

After she said that, I just shut up and obeyed.

We started walking in the direction of home. We had barely walked ten steps when we saw a young man being chased by some killers with their machetes. As they ran, they were blowing whistles to alert other killers of their prey. The piercing sound almost paralyzed me. Others were still singing as they chased him. We quickly hid ourselves in a bush and kept very quiet, listening in silent horror as the machetes sliced into his body. The boy was so terrified that he was not even able to utter one scream. When they had finished him off, they threw his body into a nearby ditch, which had been dug to collect water in the rainy season, and went on their way.

Not far from home we saw a Hutu man holding a machete standing near his house. He kept watching us and seemed to be trying to warn us not to go any further. A few moments later we could see why. Further down the road there was another Hutu who was searching for people to kill. As soon as he had gone, the first man came over to us. He recognized my grandmother and asked her if she was Stephan's wife. When she said she was, he asked where we were going. Hearing that we were on our way home, he exclaimed, "No, you can't go there. They've been searching for you. If you go there, you'll be killed."

"We don't know what else to do," my grandmother said. "Can you hide us?"

"No," he said. "I would love to but I can't. In the meeting they said they would kill any Hutu they found helping Tutsis."

We had no choice but to walk on towards our home. The familiar tracks were eerily quiet. As we made our way through the cypress woods, there was no way of knowing who was lurking in the shadows. The atmosphere was very heavy, laden with fear. All the Hutus were out looking for people to kill. They had set up roadblocks everywhere. Back on the mountain I had heard story after story of what the killers were using these roadblocks for. They were calling them "killing centers" where they herded people to kill them, gang-raping the women before brutally murdering them. Sometimes they made people wait for hours before killing them. The bodies of the people they killed were thrown, where possible, into the communal latrines (huge pits with planks across them, enclosed by brick walls) or, if these were already full, into large trenches dug for the purpose – anywhere they could find to stop the dogs getting hold of them.

Then we met Kabayiza, who was the son of our neighbor Felicita and used to work in our plantation. He was the young man to whom my father had loaned one of our cows so that his baby could have fresh milk every day, later giving him the cow's calf to keep. Seeing he was carrying a machete, we backed away, fearing the worst.

"Kabayiza," I said, "you can't be killing too?"

"No," he replied. "I've been searching for you everywhere. Your mother asked me to try and find you."

"You mean she's still alive?" I asked.

"Yes, she's still alive. She's hiding with your brothers."

"Can you take us to her?"

"No, I can't take you to where she is, but I'll take you to my house for a few hours and then we'll decide what to do."

He took us to his small house, next to his mother's, and hid all seven of us under his very small bed. His wife was away at the time visiting her family. He told us, "Don't say a word. If you hear anyone knock on the door, just stay where you are. Don't try to run away. Since I'm a Hutu no one can enter my house without my permission, I'm going to go and see what's happening."

We were all totally exhausted. We had been on the run since early morning without having anything to eat or drink. Kabayiza had left us a few boiled unpeeled sweet potatoes, but it was only enough to feed my two young cousins. We found some water in a small pot. It was very dirty but we were so thirsty we drank it. As we lay under the bed, sweating in the heat, we could hear loud bangs coming from our house down the road. When Kabayiza returned home, he told us what the banging was. "They've just finished completely destroying your home. The cows have gone, all the animals... they've taken your clothes...everything. They suspect me of hiding your father and they're coming here later to search the house. You'll have to get out of here."

"Where can we go now?" we asked. "We've nowhere to go."

"I've spoken to Simon, and he says you can go there until we decide what to do."

Simon was another of our neighbors.

"Is everyone killing?" I asked him.

"Yes," he answered, "everyone is joining in the killing."

"Even Jason and Munyentwari's sons?"

"Yes," he said.

I could not believe that these people whom I had trusted and my parents had helped so much had become killers.

As we crept through a hole in the wall of Kabayiza house past his mother's tiny house, I could see our roof tiles piled up on the floor inside.

"Where did you get these?" I asked Felicita.

"I didn't steal them," she said. "I was given them. Anyone can take anything they like from your house now."

I couldn't believe it. Felicita was a Catholic. She had

been in our house almost every day since I was born. Now she was stealing our things.

Kabayiza left us hiding in the banana plantation. He did not want to move us until the middle of the night. Even then it was very dangerous as the killers hardly slept but kept searching through the villages looking for more Tutsis to kill. The more they killed, it seemed, the more thirsty they became for blood. As we waited, we could hear them come to search Kabayiza's house. "I want to find those young girls of Bernard's," one man said. "I'm going to rape them before I kill them – especially that proud one." He was referring to my sister Mimi. The search of the small house did not take long. "I told you they're not here," Kabayiza told them when they came out. "Let's go and get a drink."

It was another couple of hours before he came back, and by then it was one or two o'clock in the morning. He told us: "They're convinced that I know where you are. I'm sure they'll come back. I need to get you away from here. Now listen: I'm going to go ahead of you. Watch me and I'll signal to you when the way is clear." By this time my two little cousins had fallen fast asleep.

Keeping our eyes on Kabayiza and watching for his signal, we crept along the hill. Crouching very low under the banana trees and cassava bushes, trying to make as little sound as we could, it seemed a very long way, although in reality it wasn't that far. When we reached Simon's house he was waiting anxiously outside. We were not allowed to go straight in, but we each had to wait until he was sure the coast was clear and then he signaled to us one at a time that we could run in. Just before I took my leave of Kabayiza, I begged him, "Please, if you see Mama or any of my brothers, can you tell them that I love them and that if we should die, we'll meet again in heaven. And please, if you can, find out if Papa is still alive."

Once again all seven of us were told to hide under urutara (a bed made of poles and ropes). On top of the bed his two children were sleeping on several layers of banana leaves. Warning us not to say a word, Simon told us that he would leave the fire burning, letting some smoke out so that passers-by would think that his wife was inside cooking. In fact he and his wife were having problems and she had gone back to live with her parents. He locked the door and went to sit outside so that he could see what was going on. Several times, as I lay awake under the bed, crushed between my sister and my auntie, in the pitch darkness, I heard men shouting to him that they were on their way to kill someone that had just been found and he should come with them. "Yeah, I'm with you. I'm with you. I'll be right after you," he shouted back.

We had arrived at his house early Sunday morning and we stayed there for three days. During that time Simon was often drunk, and we were all constantly afraid and very surprised that he did not let slip that we were there in his house. The house was sweltering hot because he kept the fire on all day and the atmosphere was very smoky, but we dare not cough or make a sound. Now and again he would give us something to eat. We tried not to drink too much because we could only go to the toilet late at night, when Simon would take us all one by one to the outside toilet, being very careful to ensure that we were not seen. From time to time the two little children would understandably get upset and start saying that they wanted to go home or that they wanted their mum or their dad. Then we would try every means possible to try and get them to be quiet again. After several days of lying under the bed in the dark, one night when I crawled out I could not see anything. I burst into tears and wailed, "I'm blind! I'm blind! I can't see anything." My aunt comforted me, "Don't worry. It's just because you've been lying in the dark for so long."

    On Tuesday Kabayiza came back, bringing the news that Mama and Beatà's children were safe and so were my brothers. He came to tell Simon that Alestude and Kiki could no longer stay at their hiding place and so he was going to bring them to where we were. After that there were nine of us, all hiding under the one small bed. From what the men said, the Hutus were hunting high and low for my brothers and had a strong suspicion that Kabayiza and Simon were protecting them. These two men did all they could to help us.

    When Kiki arrived, he was very sick with malaria. The two boys had no news of my mother. I asked Simon for a piece of paper and a pen to write a note which I hoped

Kabayiza could take to her. He had to hunt high and low to find one, but he eventually came up with a dog-eared scrap. I wrote, "Mama, I don't know whether you will survive or whether I will survive. I don't feel as if I will survive, but if you survive, remember that I love you." Mama managed to get a note through to Grandma which said, "Just be strong and know that God is with us. If we die, we will die in His arms."

Kiki and Alestude only stayed at the house for a short while before being taken to another hiding place. We kept asking Simon if there was any news of my father. One day he came back saying that he had heard my father was alive. A day or so later our hopes were crushed when he told us our father was dead. I began to cry, but my grandmother said to me, "This is no time to cry. Don't cry for the dead. Cry for the living." So we all held our tears. In fact, my father was not yet dead.

After three days Simon announced, "It's safe for you to go now. From now on they're only going to kill men and boys, so it's safe for you women to go back home."

My grandmother was immediately alarmed. "What do you mean, 'It's safe'?" How can you say we are safe when these people have killed our husbands, they have killed our sons, they have killed our brothers? How can you say that they are going to have mercy on us after they have done all that? It's a lie. You want to expose us so that we will all be killed."

He retorted, "If you don't go, I will go and call them

and tell them to come and get you. You have to go now – I don't want you to die here."

With great dignity, my grandmother turned to us and said, "Come, we'll go to home (Grandfather's house) and wait there for our death."

Chapter 5
Waiting for Death

All that was left of my grandparents' house was a shell. The roof was gone and so were the windows and doors. Everything had been taken apart from my grandfather's books, which lay strewn across the floor. Sitting in the midst of the desolation was my grandfather. He looked very thin and full of despair. He had thought we were all already dead. Although he was glad to see us, his face remained emotionless. After we had embraced him, he told us that time and time again he had been taken to the killing center to be killed, but each time they had brought him back again. Because he was such a respected member of the community, they kept saying that they were going to leave him till the end. From what he had seen he was the only Tutsi man left alive.

For the next four days we waited for death. The Hutus knew we were there, but they also knew we wouldn't be going anywhere. During those days we had very little to eat or drink but, since it was the rainy season, we drank the water we collected on banana leaves or in our cupped hands. When he could, our grandfather's herdsman Martin brought us milk from his cows. When there was no one around, we would creep into the surrounding plantations and gather any vegetables we could find, cooking them in an old broken pot. So often the meager meals we were able to cook were just heartlessly tipped onto the ground by any Hutu killer who happened to be passing at that moment.

On the second day we were joined by my father's two cousins who arrived in a dreadful state – they could barely walk. As soon as they saw us, they collapsed in floods of tears. They told us that they had been raped over and over again by different killers. Sarah was twenty-one and Fina was nineteen.

On the third day – Tuesday – Mama arrived with Beatà's two boys. The message we had heard from Simon that the women were no longer going to be killed had been put around the whole village and so all the women and their children were emerging from their hiding places. Somehow Mama had found out that we were all together at Grandfather's house and had come to join us there. She was absolutely exhausted. The three of them had been hiding at the home of Rwubusisi, one of our neighbors who was an old friend of the family. Mama was godmother to one of his children.

In the middle of that night we were all scared out of our wits by a man dropping down into the house from the roof. This man no longer looked human. He had the face of a man who was utterly terrified. So many people had died that I thought it must be a ghost (not that I have seen one but this is an expression in our language that means a terrible look). We gradually realized it was my father. We were amazed that he was still alive, but shocked by what we saw. He looked terrible. He had lost so much weight; his hair was long and unkempt, and he had grown a beard; his clothes were filthy and he had no shoes. He too had been in hiding, we discovered, but having been sent away by his protector, he had been hiding among the rooftops – they were often overhung by banana trees and their broad leaves provided secluded hiding places. He stayed with us for the rest of the night but then he left. Since they were saying that the women were no longer going to be killed, he thought we would be safer if he was not there. He continued to hide among the rooftops, watching us from a distance.

The next day Mama asked Kabayiza to go and fetch my brothers so that we could all be together. From somewhere she found some dresses and told the boys to put them on. Of course they complained like mad, but she made them do it. There was the faintest glimmer of hope that what they were saying was true, but in our heart of hearts we knew that the killing was not going to stop plus my brothers were known by their killers as boys anyways. There were now sixteen of us, waiting together.

That same afternoon the killers came for us. It was Wednesday, May 4. We heard their songs before we saw them. They were a disgusting sight. Vying with each other for the reputation of the fiercest killer they would use banana leaves to strap the hands of their victims around their head or around their wrists. Many of them would also drink human blood to show off their skills in killing.

As we were herded out of the house and onto the street, we met fifty or sixty other women and children who had also been rounded up. Among them were some boys who, like my brothers, had been forced by their mothers to wear dresses. We were being taken to the roadblock they were using as a killing center, about a ten-minute walk away.

Brandishing his Bible in the air, my grandfather, who was the only man among the crowd, went to the head of the desolate column of people with us following close behind him. "Sing," he urged everyone. "Sing, because this is the last time you're going to sing. They may kill our bodies, but they can never kill our spirits. We're going to heaven!" Then he started up a rousing hymn, and many people joined in. While with my mouth I was forming the words, in my heart I was screaming out to God, "Why have you abandoned us, God? Why are you allowing these people to do this to us?" As far as I was concerned God had stopped listening.

We had only gone a short way when the killers halted the crowd of people. They said to a fourteen-year-old youth carrying a blood-stained machete, "We haven't eaten yet today and we're hungry. You take this cockroaches to iseta (the killing center) while we go and get something to eat. We'll meet you there later. They won't go anywhere." This boy had been in the same primary-school class as me. Seventy or eighty people allowed this fourteen-year-old boy to lead them to their death. We were weak from hunger and exhaustion. We were in despair. We had nowhere to run.

When we reached the killing center my heart almost stopped. There was blood everywhere. Several hundred women and children were already there. We sat down with all the others and waited for death.

When the killers came back, they talked among themselves about how they were going to kill so many people and then dispose of their bodies.

"We're going to need a grenade to finish all these people off," one said. "It'll take too long to kill them all."

"What are you talking about?" another man said. "Killing Tutsis isn't hard work," and with that he began to hit out at a woman who was sitting right next to me and she fell over on top of me. I really thought that my moment to die had come.

"Stop it! Stop it!" another man intervened. "We can't kill them yet. There are too many of them. We have no way of getting rid of their bodies. You know, those Tutsis smell so bad. We need to get hold of a grenade first."

"A grenade?" the man who wanted to get on with it argued. "Tutsis don't deserve grenades or bullets. Have they paid for them?" Then turning to the crowd, he shouted, "If any of you Tutsis has money, come forward. If you pay us 5000 Francs[ii*] we will shoot you, instead of killing you with a machete."

But no one had any money. After that the leader of the killers told us to go away, saying they would kill us another day. "They are ours," he told his group of men. "We can have them anytime we want."

When we got back to the house we were all starving hungry. Before they had taken us, my grandmother had cooked some vegetables which she had tried to hide. By the time we got back, they were gone. We were so hungry that we chewed on banana leaves.

A day later, on Friday, a woman came to the house to gloat over us. She was a Tutsi but she was married to a Hutu and her sons were very heavily involved in the killing. She said all sorts of insulting things to my grandmother and made horrible threats about what the Hutus were going to do to us. My grandmother said to her, "Today it is us; tomorrow it may be you."

Later the same day one of Kiki's friend who was a Hutu came to the house. He was very agitated. He had just come from a meeting held by the killers. The following day, May 7, the assassinated Hutu president was due to be buried and the killers, wanting to mark the day, were intending to kill all the remaining Tutsi women and children on the day. Their blood was to be "a cover" for the president's grave. Asking that we didn't tell anyone that it was he who had told us of the Hutus' plan, he begged, "They're coming to kill you tomorrow. You've got to make a run for it." When he had gone, Kiki wanted to try to escape, but my grandfather persuaded him against it. "There's nowhere to run. If you try to escape they will certainly kill you. Stay here, and let's die together. At least then we will all be buried together and if anyone in our family survives then they can be able to pick our pieces together."

The hours dragged slowly by, with few words being exchanged between us. Physically, mentally and emotionally exhausted, we were all in an extremely traumatized state – already more dead than alive. Only Kiki, with the resources of his youth, tried to break the tension with the occasional joke. Knowing that my grandmother had dug up some cassava, he urged her to cook it, saying, "Let me eat today because tomorrow I won't be able to." I sometimes wonder why we didn't run away, but I think it was because death was already in our heads.

That night as a family we all huddled together in the pitch darkness in the tiny, now roofless storeroom of Grandfather's house. Led by Grandfather, we knelt together and repented of our sins before God. Knowing that we were to die the next day, we could not sleep. We just waited for death.

In a corner of my heart there was still a vestige of hope that by some miracle we might be saved. We had heard somehow that the Rwandan Patriotic Front (RPF) soldiers were advancing and that they had saved some people in Kigali. As we sat waiting in the small hours of the night I said to my mother, "Do you think that a miracle might happen and the RPF might come and rescue us?"

"Don't talk to me about those stupid fighters," she said angrily. "They are the ones to blame for all this trouble.

They brought this upon us and they can't even finish what they started."

"Mama," I said, "don't speak against them. They might still come and save us." I knew this was spoken out of frustration, anger and powerlessness that she felt of not being able to save her own children and that her hope in the RPF soldiers was fading away. Knowing that she had already been told when exactly she would be killed.

Very early the next morning, about 3 o'clock, we suddenly heard a great deal of noise and commotion coming from our nearest neighbors' house, twenty or thirty meters away. There was a family with young children living there, as well as a woman who was nine-months pregnant. She was the one I had seen on the mountain when we were trying to escape. The babies and young children were screaming with terror. There were the sounds of clubs crashing down on people's heads and machetes slicing into their bodies. I heard one child cry out, "Please forgive me. Please forgive me. I promise I will never be a Tutsi again." Gradually the screams subsided as one by one they were all murdered. We heard the dull thud as each body was thrown into the toilet of the house and the door slammed shut. The pregnant woman was obviously not yet dead and we heard her moans but i guess they left her to die or were rushing to come to us. After a few minutes, silence. Shaken to the core with the horror of what we had heard, we huddled together. Trembling. Terrified.

Next they came to us.

First came a young man. He was covered in blood and the machete in his hand was still dripping with blood. We recognized him. He had been in the soccer team Papa had formed for my brothers and the local lads in the area. He looked at us. Then he turned round and went back to the other killers who had surrounded the house. "There's no one here," he told them. "They've all gone."

Then the leader of the killers came into the house and saw us. His name was Gakuba. He was an elder in the Seventh Day Adventist church. When we saw him, we all immediately covered our faces with our hands. The sight of him was horrifying. So full of blood. So much evil in his eyes. So much hatred. And Gakuba had made himself a name as an unforgiving and no merciless killer. While there was no such thing as a good death, if you were captured by him, or his friend and co-killer Kimonyo, you would be guaranteed an awful death. "So they are not here, are they? You say you didn't see all these snakes and cockroaches (we were not human to them) cowering in here?"

"No, I didn't see them. It's too dark in here to see." The young man tried to sound convincing.

"Well, if you want to make up for your little mistake, you'd better kill at least ten of them."

"I will, I will," the young man stuttered. "But I tell you I didn't see them."

"Outside!" he ordered us.

My grandfather got up and we all followed, keeping as close to him as we could. Now we had to face our killers.

My grandfather had his Bible in his hands. He fell to his knees and began to implore the men for mercy. "Why are you killing us? We have lived side by side with you as your brothers and sisters. What have we done? I taught you as I taught my own children. Jesus Christ told us that we should love one another. Why are you condemning yourselves by having our blood on your hands? Why don't you just forgive us?"

On and on he went, begging them, pleading with them. Finally Gakuba said, "Stop wasting our time, old man. We've got too much work to do today." Then turning to one of his men, he said, "Check the toilet and see how much room there is in there." The man came back saying that it was already full.[iii*]

Again my grandfather cried out, "Why can't you forgive us?"

"We will spare you and your wife, because you are old," Gakuba relented. "But all the rest of these snakes will have to die. But be quick and make up your mind. You are wasting our time."

"If you kill my children and my grandchildren, what is the point of me living?" my grandfather said. "What is the use of a tree without its branches? I choose to die with my children and my grandchildren."

Then he asked that we be allowed to pray together

for the last time. "What's the point?" they said. "You Tutsis have no God. God has forsaken you." But they let him have his wish. We all knelt together as he prayed. Before he had even finished, some of the men grabbed hold of my mother and started tearing at her clothes, ready to rape her. The little four-year-old was on her back.

"Why are you raping me in front of my children?" she screamed. "Kill them first so that at least they do not have to witness that, and then you can do whatever you like to me." She did not want us to suffer any more than we were already suffering. And to this day I admire my mother's strength to even voice that. Today, as a mother myself, I have no idea how I would respond in front of my kids if faced with such a situation. My mother was an incredibly strong and courageous woman, but it breaks my heart to consider her agony as she sought to protect her children.

"If that's the way you want it," said Gakuba.

At that moment one of the killers came back and told them they had found a place to dump our bodies. They took us a short distance from the house where, on the edge of my grandparents' banana plantation, there was a long, thin trench about a meter deep, in which rain water had begun to collect. As we walked, some of the killers followed us while others went on ahead, but my grandfather ordered us to sing again. It was a hymn from a Catholic song book proclaiming that we belong to the heavens where we will be happy for eternity. To this day I have not stopped thinking what an amazing and Godly man my grandfather was. I perhaps already knew this as a child, but as an adult now, it touches my heart to know that he was hated all his life yet did not curse his killers, not even on the day he was killed and buried. He was a man who was not changed or affected by circumstances, problems, and troubles. Even death itself did not take his kindness. My grandfather still believed in God and showed the world that death had no power over his spirit.

We were then ordered into the pit and Gakuba shouted, "Now choose which weapon you want to kill you! And hurry up. We have got so much to do today." As I looked up at the twenty or more killers crowding around the edge of the trench, in my head I was screaming out, "This can't be happening! I know you. You are my neighbors. You can't be about to kill us." I looked at the terrifying weapons they were carrying. There were machetes, knives, spears, clubs, spades and sticks studded with nails. They were all already drenched in blood. Not that I was fine with any weapon but it was the machetes and the knives I most feared. I had seen people killed with clubs – they hit them once or twice on the back of the head, the brains came out, and it was all over. I knew one of the men carrying a club – he was a young man called John.

I heard my mother say, "Death is death. I will not choose."

I said, "I choose John. Please don't kill me with

anything else."

All the young children were crying, but the rest of us were silent. That moment was beyond any emotion.

We were all told to lie face-down on the bottom of the trench. It was not wide enough to lie across it, so we all had to lie lengthwise, our bodies overlapping each other in the confined space. Just as my grandfather was saying again, "Why don't you forgive us?" he was hit with a stick by Gatoya, one of the men who had wanted to rape my mother, and he fell forward. As I looked across at my mother I saw a machete coming down onto her neck and her head falling to the side. Then I saw them cut off her leg. She made no sound. I heard my brothers cry out, "Please forgive me, please forgive me" and then screaming with searing pain. I put my hands over my face. At that moment the club hit me. My tongue came out of my mouth and I could feel blood pouring down my chin. Then I was plunged into unconsciousness.

I don't know how long I was unconscious for. When I came round again, I heard the killers talking. They were talking and joking about how long it took Tutsis to die, even the old and the very young. They were stepping over the bodies, looking to see if anyone was still alive. Of course, they were piled on top of one another and it was not easy for them to see. My little cousin was lying next to me. I could hear her moaning gently. "This one's not dead yet," a man standing over her shouted. Thud. His weapon came down on her and her blood splattered over me. Then I heard John's voice. "I'm going to cut these feet off," he said. The feet he was talking about were mine. A moment later I felt excruciating pain but I did not move a muscle or make a sound. I did not even take a breath. He did not take the whole foot off but just slashed the back of both my heels and may be got my sister who was next to me too. They were working in a hurry because they wanted to move on. When they thought that everyone was dead, they filled in the trench again, so that the bodies were covered with a thick layer of earth, and went away. I did not know at the time that my father had watched his whole family being killed. I thought to myself that he may have been smart enough to save himself and go. And that maybe he would come down after the killers had left to save me and that I would at least have a father since my whole family was gone and that I would be alright if I had him with me. But I was so wrong. My father could not move or leave as what he had lived for was gone. His entire family was killed in front of his face, there was no reason for him to live anymore, and he had no idea I was still breathing anyway.

Chapter 6
"You Will Suffer But You Will Live"

I was lying face down in mud and blood. Many people have asked me how I survived but I tell them I do not know. The only answer I can give is that God saved me. I know that my Aunt Martha was also buried alive. My head was lying on her side, and I could hear her groans and feel her body convulsing. I called to her but there was no response. Then the groans stopped and I knew she had died. She only survived a few minutes. But I lay there entombed for something like thirteen or fourteen hours.

I could not move. The earth pressed heavily on my body. The smell of blood filled my nostrils and the taste of blood filled my mouth. As the hours passed, an intense cold crept over me. I tried to shout for help but no sound seemed to come out of my mouth. As I lay there in the pitch blackness, with the dead bodies of my loved ones all around me, I prayed, "Lord, if you take me out of this grave, I will serve you all the days of my life and I will be a nun." As a child who was raised catholic I thought the best way to serve God and be a godly woman would be to become a nun.

The hours passed, but death did not come. It must have been about three or four in the afternoon. I had lost sense of time, but I then felt a pressure on the ground above my head. Someone must have been walking over the filled-in trench. Then they stood still. Summoning every remaining ounce of energy in my body, I tried to shout for one last time. After a few seconds the person moved off. Or perhaps it was a stray dog that was attracted by the smell of the bodies.

Minutes later though, I heard voices and the sound of digging. At first they dug in the wrong place and found only a corpse, but they persisted and eventually they found me. Digging with their spades, they uncovered the top part of my body. My rescuers were two Hutus, Lambert and Nshokeye. Lambert was a young man of nineteen who used to work for my grandfather. He had come to our grave, knowing that someone might still be alive. It was well known that sometimes the Hutu killers deliberately buried people alive to make their death even more horrific. Lambert really loved my grandfather and the whole family.

He had consistently refused to have any part in the killing of the Tutsis, despite having been threatened, beaten and attacked with machetes by his fellow Hutus. As a result he walked with a limp. For years after my survival I had thought that Lambert had heard the shout which I was not even sure had come out of my mouth and had run to fetch the other man. But years later, I actually discovered from our neighbor Nirere that she was the one who heard my voice. Terrified that it might have been a ghost, she went to tell Lambert. Now I understand that the Lord used this poor widow, and it is to her that I owe my life (unfortunately Nirere has passed way and I have no way to pay her back for her heroic action). The other man was Nshokeye, the son of the Tutsi woman who – can it have really just been two days before? – had come to gloat over our family. Perhaps Lambert thought that because Nshokeye had a Tutsi mother he would show some mercy to the poor wretch that had managed to cheat death. He was wrong, however. Seeing I was indeed still alive, Nshokeye reached for his machete, intending to cut off my head.

"Kill me," I said. "Go ahead and kill me. I want to die."

As Nshokeye raised his machete, Lambert rammed his whole body against him and threatened, "Up till now I haven't killed anyone, but if you touch her, I swear I will kill you!"

"She is asking to die," the other man said.

"Leave her," Lambert warned, his voice bristling with rage.

Seeing that he was in deadly earnest, Nshokeye let his machete fall to his side. The two men then tried to drag me out of the earth by my arms. I thought my body was going to be torn in two. I was covered in blood and mud – my eyes, my nose, my hair, everything... Congealed blood covered the wound at the back of my head and the gashes on my heels. My head was swollen.

As the earth finally released my body, I ended up in the arms of Nshokeye. At that very moment there was the sound of singing and shouting and a roaming band of Hutu killers came into view. These men were not from the area and had a reputation of being even more vicious than the local killers. They never showed any mercy. "Shh, keep quiet," Nshokeye hissed, throwing me down on the mound of earth they had created with their digging. The two men ran off, warning, "Don't ever tell anyone who rescued you."

The five killers surveyed my crumpled, filthy, bloodied body. "What are you? Are you a human being or a ghost?" asked one killer, who wore the hands of his victims displayed as trophies around his head.

I wiped the mud from my eyes and said, "I am a human being." I was not afraid any more.

"Are you a human being or a ghost?" another demanded.

"I am a human being," I repeated.

They asked the question again and again, hardly able to believe the answer I was giving them. Witchcraft was so much a part of their way of life that they could well believe that I was the spirit of one of their victims. Then they wanted to know where I had come from. When I told them I had come out of the trench a few meters away, they asked me who had dug me out.

"I dug myself out," I told them.

"Finish her off," the leader ordered.

"Yes, kill me," I said. "I want to die."

"You are already dead," they kept saying.

None of the men wanted to kill me, each saying that he did not kill ghosts. While the killers stood talking, deliberating among themselves whether I was a ghost or a human being, I caught a snatch of a conversation between some men a short distance away. What I heard devastated me. One man said, "Have you heard what happened this morning?"

"No, what happened?" came the reply.

"We killed Bernard. All this time he was hiding up on the roof of his father's house."

All hope that my father was still alive was finally extinguished. All hope that I might see him again one day was obliterated. As the killers turned to leave, saying, "Just leave her to die. She'll be dead in twenty minutes," I pleaded with them again, "Are you going without killing me? Just kill me, I want to die." They just laughed and went on their way.

As soon as they were out of sight, Lambert, who had been watching from a distance, came over to me, bringing me a cup of milk. "Thank God you're still alive," he said. "I felt sure they would kill you." He told me that Nirere, who lived nearby, and was actually the lady who had told him about me being in the ditch had agreed to take me for the night. She had three young children, two boys and a girl. He went a short way ahead to make sure the coast was clear and motioned for me to follow. I tried to stand but I immediately collapsed back onto the ground. Lambert put me over his shoulder and carried me to Nirere's house.

When Nirere saw me, she burst into tears. "Frida, what have they done to you? What have they done? What has become of us Hutus? We are like animals! We are bringing a curse on our nation."

I was too weak and exhausted to speak. She hid me under an enormous stack of bean plants that she had drying in her tiny house. I could hear rats moving about. Normally I would have been terrified, but now I was past caring about anything.

Soon after Lambert left, saying that he would come back in the morning. Unbeknown to us, we had been seen entering Nirere's house. Moments later four killers came into the house, demanding that she hand me over to them. She vehemently denied any knowledge of me, saying, "You know I hate Tutsis. And if I wasn't able to save her grandfather Stephan, whom I worked for and who was my good neighbor for so many years, what chance would I have of saving her?"

Refusing to take her word for it, they demanded to search the house, threatening that if they found me, they would kill her and her children.

"Go ahead," she said, "but you won't find her."

I could hear them rattling and banging as they searched through the house. Not finding me, they pounced upon the huge pile of bean plants. Angrily they plunged their spears into the stack. With each thrust of their spear they shouted out, "You mean she's not in here?", "She's not in here?" I did not move a muscle. Amazingly, no spear touched me.

They were convinced I was in that house somewhere

and refused to give up. They were starting to dismantle the pile, angrily tossing the plants all over the floor of the house, when one of their leaders came to find them. "What are you doing wasting your time looking for that girl?" he shouted. "Don't you realize that those Tutsi rebels, those cockroaches, are advancing towards this area? If we don't finish off the rest of those Tutsis today, it will be too late. Stop wasting time. Come on."

"We'll be back," they warned Nirere as they reluctantly left. Fearing for the safety of her children, as soon as they had gone far enough, she sent me away. Not knowing where I could go, desperately weak and hardly able to walk, I sat down on the ground a short distance from her house. Seeing me there, she came out and shouted at me, "Get right away from here. If they catch you anywhere near here, they will come and kill my children and me. Go away." I could not believe that someone who in few moments ago had mercy on me and cried because of me would then send me away, but it was a time of friends turning their backs on us. You could not trust anyone anymore. Years later, I went back to visit Nirere together with my friends James and Tina from England and thanked her for doing even what she had done. One may think why thank her? After all she sent you away! Yet I also think that if she had not simply called for my help when I was still burred with my family, I probably would be dead and forgotten. And you would not be reading this book today and the story of how my family died would have simply not been told. I recognized that the fear of losing her own children to the hands of her fellow Hutus was very real. After all, she had been threatened and had to make difficult decisions. She was of course not proud of it when I visited her and she asked me to forgive her. I could not blame her for this but thanked her for what she had done.

    Each step was excruciatingly painful, but I got as far away from the house as I could. The whole night I lay by the edge of a banana plantation. I did not care whether I lived or died. I did not sleep. I just lay there, listening to the never-ending shouts of the killers whose appetite for blood was still not satisfied. I don't know how it found me, but my father's dog Bobby came and lay by my side as if it was trying to protect me.

    Early the next morning I realized that I was too exposed and that I needed to find somewhere to hide. Remembering how Mama had hidden us all in the bushes I found a huge bush and crept underneath it. The dog was still following me. I tried to chase it away as I knew that the dog will make my presence very obvious, yet it would not leave me. A couple of hours later the bush was surrounded by people. The word had got round that I had survived – probably Nshokeye had been talking – and my survival was adding fire to a worry that was growing among the Hutu killers. With the increasing pressure of the impending arrival of the RPF Inkotanyi, they were beginning to fear reprisals. They were well aware that any surviving Tutsis would be able to tell the story of their atrocities. "These people who aren't being finished off properly," they were saying to one another, "are the very ones who will tell the Tutsi cockroaches what we have done. We have got to find them and kill them all so they can't talk." Noticing that my father's dog was staying close to one particular bush, they put two and two together and realized I was in there.

The dog was making a terrible noise barking at them all. "If you don't come out," they shouted, "we'll set fire to the bush and you'll burn to death." I didn't really care if they set fire to the bush. To me burning to death seemed preferable to being attacked with a machete or knife. But, as they were shouting, they were thrusting their machetes and their sticks into the bush and they were gradually getting closer and closer to me. My fear of machetes forced me out of the bush. You knew very well that you may die yet at the same time hoped they will have mercy and let you go one more time. When I emerged they could not believe they had expended so much effort looking for such a pitiful creature. "You mean we've spent all this time looking for this wretched girl?" they said to one another. "She's half dead already. Just leave her to die." Warning the people who lived in the area including Nirere not to give me anything to eat or drink, they left me.

Just by the bush there was a large rock. I sat myself on the rock and waited. There was no point in trying to hide – everyone knew where I was. Again and again, as I sat there – alone and exposed for all the world to see – the realization that I was never going to see my family again hit me. My brain refused to take it in. I kept hoping I would wake up and realize it was just a horrible nightmare. There were no tears. There was no pain. I was too numb for that. There was just a huge chasm opening up inside me. As I sat there grappling with reality, one thought kept going round and round in my head: "You will suffer but you will live... You will suffer but you will live..." I tried to dismiss it. It was a crazy thought. How could I survive? I was all alone in the world. The Hutus were still hell bent on wiping the Tutsis off the face of the earth. My whole family was dead, and I wanted to die too. Nevertheless, the thought would not leave me.

After about half an hour a tall, thin man carrying a machete and a big bag came over to me. I recognized him as a neighbor of ours, whose small land-holding lay on the opposite side of the valley. His face was very distinctive as one of his eyes was permanently half-shut. His name was Vitale. He said, "Come with me. I'm going to take you to my house. I'll carry you in this bag so that no one will see you." I did not trust him. I thought he was going to take me somewhere and rape me. But, perhaps swayed by the voice that was telling me I was going to survive, I went with him. And anyway, what option did I have? I refused point blank, however, to be put in the bag, fearing that I would suffocate inside it. Instead he found a small tree for me to hide behind. So now, half dead, I was being asked to carry a tree.

Vitale had already spoken with Nirere, the woman

who had hidden me for a few hours the previous day, and she gave me some of her clothes to put over me. When we arrived at his house, his grown-up son was there. He was absolutely furious with his father for endangering the family's lives by taking me to their home and threatened to kill me. His father told him that if he laid a hand on me, he would kill him.

Vitale told me that I could stay at his home but that he would have to tell the men in charge that I was there – otherwise they would kill him. Then we would just have to wait and see what happened. Seeing the despair on my face, he tried to comfort me by saying, "Don't give up hope. You're not completely alone. Your grandfather's brother is still alive. They beat him unconscious and they intended to bury him alive, but while they were looking for somewhere to put him, someone stole his body. My brother has been hiding him at his house. It's going to be over soon. You might still come out of this alive." I told him, "Even if I live, I will have no hope, because all my family is dead."

For the next six weeks I remained in hiding at Vitale's house. During the day I would hide in the house. Knowing that the house might be searched at any time, at night he would hide me outside in his banana plantation, often changing the hiding place. Most of the time I slept in a small hole in the ground which he had dug. Once I was inside he would cover it with banana leaves and no one would ever have known there was a human being inside. Lying in the hole for hours on end my ears were deafened by the sound of my heart beating. When someone eventually came to fetch me, my legs were so numb that I could hardly walk.

One night while I was enclosed in my hidey-hole, I heard a dog nearby and there was a terrible smell. When I removed a few of the banana leaves to see what was causing the smell, I was horrified by what I saw. The dog was gnawing at my grandfather's arm. I could recognize his watch and the jacket he was wearing when he died. Dogs were digging out and feeding themselves on human bodies in the whole country.

I never knew whether Vitale had actually told the Hutu killers that he was sheltering me, but they never stopped looking for me and there were a couple of close shaves. On one occasion a very persistent man from the Batwa tribe called Ngamije came to the house. Rwandans always used to joke that these people, who made up only one per cent of the nation, would blow with the wind as far as their allegiance was concerned. This man had been promised that he would be promoted to the rank of major in the army if he filled a very large pit right by the primary school for disabled children with the bodies of Tutsi women and girls, and he was determined to do it.

He came to Vitale's house during the day but for some reason I was hiding in my tiny hole in the banana plantation. He spent the whole day searching, first the house and then the plantation. Totally frustrated he was wildly chopping down banana leaves and these were falling over my hiding place, making it even more secure. I could see him through the leaves. At one point he climbed an avocado tree to try and get a better vantage point, but to no avail. Eventually, at about three in the afternoon, he gave up and went away.

On another occasion they came unexpectedly in the middle of the night to search the house and, unusually, I was sleeping inside. Vitale was very angry that he had not been warned that they were coming and at first he tried to stop them entering the house. When they demanded to be allowed to search, he insisted that I had already been apprehended and killed, but they were having none of it. Pushing past him, they began to search the house. His two daughters pulled me down on the floor where they were sleeping on banana leaves and lay on top of me, pulling the cover over them. One of the men pulled the cover down and shone a torch into their faces, but he did not see me.

I do not know why Vitale was so kind to me. Perhaps he was using me as a sort of insurance policy in case things ever went the other way. After I had been at his house for a while he also took in a young Tutsi man Matthew who had somehow managed to survive. I have since come to understand that, at the same time that he was sheltering me, he was still going out every night with his machete to kill Tutsis. I only knew that, on his return, he would always wash his machete before he came into the house and spoke to me.

I had two visitors at Vitale's house. The first was Nirere, the woman who had sheltered me for a short time. After I had been there a week or two, she came to ask where my father kept the second-hand clothes he used to supply to the market-traders in Nyanza and where his "other treasures" were (by that she meant money). I did not know and I would not have told her anyway. And I think she was being used by other people to come and ask all that.

The second visitor was much more welcome. It was Lambert who had saved me. He came to see me several times. I told him about the voice I had heard in my head telling me over and over again, "You will suffer but you will live." After the genocide was over, he wrote me a letter in which he told me that he had felt like an angel when he had rescued me. He could not understand how I could have been buried in that grave for so many hours and yet survive. Although he was not a believer, he wrote, "I always wonder why God saved your life and what purpose He has for you.

Chapter 7

Facing Life Alone

On July 4, the RPF took Kigali. The government fell and the tide in Rwanda turned. Bombs began to fall over Nyanza as the Inkotanyi forces drew nearer. I could not contain my joy that I was going to be saved, and this made Vitale's daughter very angry. She urged her father to kill me. "If you don't kill her," she said, "she will betray us all to the Tutsis." Vitale refused, saying, "No, I can't kill her. Actually, it wasn't me who saved her – it was God. God saved her."

The Hutus began to flee, among them Vitale and his family. He explained to me that it was too dangerous to take me with them because I would be killed by other fleeing Hutus. However, staying put was also dangerous. Although most of the local Hutus had now left, the area was still full of retreating Hutu militiamen who were intent on killing anyone they encountered: both surviving Tutsis and any lingering Hutus, whom they would suspect of collaboration. Vitale told me to stay in the house until I was sure the area was in the hands of the Tutsis.

The next couple of days were terrifying. Our valley, with Vitale's house on one side and my family home on the other, lay right in the middle of the advancing Tutsis, who had reached as far as my old primary school, and the retreating Hutu army, who were held up near my grandfather's house. All night bombs and gunshots flew overhead, and I lived in fear that the house might be hit at any moment. Some food had been left in the house, which I cooked during the day. When there was a lull, I would run over to Vitale's brother's house next door to take food to my grandfather's brother, who had also been abandoned, coming back as quickly as I could.

After four days Vitale and his family returned. I think he must have reconsidered and decided that his best option was to use me as a safety valve. He took me outside and spoke to me privately. "Listen," he said, "you and I need to do business. I saved your life, now you're going to save me and my family. I'm not a bad man. I haven't killed anybody. You are going to talk to the Tutsis and tell them what I have done for you."

Soon after his return one of my father's Tutsi friends who had managed to survive, came to Vitale's house. He had heard I was there and wanted me to go with him to my old primary school, Gatagara, where all the Tutsi survivors were being taken for safety. "All the other orphans are there," he said. The mention of the word "orphan" provoked a very strong reaction in me. "I am not an orphan," I said. "I'm not going to go there until I find out if any members of my family are still alive. I don't want to go there." He left without me. I later discovered that all the Tutsis sheltering in the school had been kidnapped by Hutus and slaughtered, only few survived that attack.

Throughout the whole time I had been living with

Vitale, there had also been a young man there. He was a twenty-year-old called Janvier and was related to Vitale on his mother's side, but his father was a Tutsi. Janvier had come to live with Vitale at the start of the genocide, but since he was unknown in the area and all that people knew about him was that he was a relative, he was not in hiding and no one bothered him. Hearing that Nyanza was into RPF hands, he and I decided that we should try and make our way there. I said goodbye to Vitale and promised him that I would speak to the RPF soldiers and tell them what he had done for me. However, if he had done other things where I did not see I was not going to stop what his consequences was going to be with the law. I shall always be grateful to Vitale for the care he showed in protecting me.

The one-and-a-half-hour walk to Nyanza was terrifying. Not only was there the deafening sound of bombs exploding first on one side and then on the other and the danger from stray bullets, but all along the road there were cruelly disfigured corpses. Some had clearly lain there for weeks; others were more recent. The smell was terrible. The whole way we did not meet a single living person.

As soon as we arrived in Nyanza, Janvier and his brother whom we had picked on our way to Nyanza left me. They both wanted to join the RPF army and fight the rest of the battle and stop the Hutus from killing people. As we parted, I urged Janvier, when it was all over, to go back and look after Vitale's family.

After the two left, I did not know what to do. I tried a few houses where I heard they were taking in children who were on their own. At each door on which I knocked, I received the same response: they were full and could not take anyone else. I felt very alone and very vulnerable. I was filthy dirty, having worn the same clothes for three months; my hair was so encrusted that it had turned yellow and was ridden with lice. I was also suffering from malaria and for some days had been vomiting stuff mixed with blood in it. It all suddenly became too much. I sat down by the side of the road and began to cry. And having started I could not stop. As I sat there sobbing uncontrollably, the world carried on around me. It began to rain.

After I had been sitting there for some time, my tears still flowing, a young man came over to me and asked me what was wrong. At first I could not speak. I could not stop crying. Trying to comfort me he told me he could take me to a place where they would look after me. Through my sobs I told him that I had tried everywhere and they were all completely full. He said he knew a man who he thought might be able to help me.

He took me with him to find him. When we found the man, whose name was Musoni, he asked me about myself. I told him who my father and my grandfather were and he said that he knew them. In fact, he told me that he and some of the RPF soldiers had gone to my grandfather's house hoping to save us but they had arrived too late.

"Are you the only person who survived?" he asked.

"I'm not sure," I replied. "There's a chance that one of the others might also have survived, in the same way I did." At this point I think I was still moving back and forth from reality to denial and back again.

He wanted to take me to stay with a friend of his, who, I discovered, lived in one of the houses I had already tried. When I explained that she had already told me she had too many children to care for, he said that as his friend he was sure she would take me in, which she did. As soon as I got to her house, I went straight to bed, without eating or having a bath. I was just too exhausted to do anything else.

The next three weeks passed in a blur. At first I was very sick, but as I recovered from the malaria, the full effects of the trauma set in. I kept to myself and avoided speaking whenever possible – I definitely couldn't cope with the endless teenage chatter of the other girls about their boyfriends. The woman who had taken me in, although very kind, had her hands more than full trying to care for so many in such difficult circumstances.

In the months that followed I gradually began to discover, one by one, which of the members of my wider family had survived. First of all, I discovered that one of the girls living in the same house was the daughter of my father's cousin. Her name was Terry. Her brother, who had been studying in Belgium when the genocide started, had been searching for his family through the Red Cross. They found his mother first in a place called Ruhango, and she directed them to the Nyanza area where some of her children had been when the genocide started. When the Red Cross arrived to take her to her mother and her two surviving sisters, the girl refused to go without me. So I went with her to join her mother, who was living at the home of a Catholic priest, and we all stayed there. It meant so much to me to discover that some of my family had survived. I had thought I would never see any member of my family again. Later we were tracked down by another cousin, Magnifique, who was equally delighted to know that she was not alone.

After a few weeks of living with the Catholic priest, my father's cousin met a man she knew who was a major in the RPF. He took us all to live in a place called Byumba on the Ugandan border where he had a large property consisting of several houses. We lived in one of the houses and in another house were billeted some of his soldiers. In the aftermath of the genocide, when there was so much confusion, desolation and despair and no one was sure if they would find any members of their family left alive, people would open up their homes to anyone in need. It was a relief to be away from the main areas where the fighting had taken place. There was still some shooting going on and in many places there was the danger of unexploded bombs.

One day I was very frightened when a man in a soldier's uniform came to the house asking for me. I didn't recognize him, and the Major had instilled in us all to be very wary of strangers even if they claimed to be relatives, because it was not uncommon for children to be kidnapped by Hutus and murdered. I couldn't understand why anyone should come looking for me. I said to the man, "I'm not even going to talk to you because I don't recognize you." The man burst out laughing. It was dark, we had only one or two candles lighting the whole house. Hearing his voice, I suddenly recognized that it was my Uncle Narcisse, the elder of my mother's two brothers who had joined the RPF, and I just jumped up into his arms and started crying. The memory that popped in my mind of him was that he had visited just a few months before the genocide and had taken some pictures of us. He loved my mother so much and so did her whole family. I tried to tell him that everyone else was dead, but he just said, "Shh, Frida. We'll talk later." He could not stay long as his battalion was passing through the area. Before he left, he told me that his brother was also searching for me. But as he left I was not sure I would ever see him again or that his brother would ever find me. I was even more worried that I had raised my hopes and would not last.

My mother's other brother came to see me some months later. By this time my father's cousin and her family had been rehoused, but I was still living with the Major. Aware that I was extremely traumatized he wanted me to remain in the very secure environment of his home. On this occasion, too, I greeted my visitor very warily. My father's cousin had sent him to the house and he was with two other family members. They stood knocking at the door.

"Who is it?" I asked through the door.

"Open the door and see," came the voice.

"I never open the door to strangers," I replied. "If you do not say your name, I won't open the door."

"Even if I say my name, you won't recognize me," he said. "Just open the door and see." I could hear the emotion in his voice.

I went to call one of the soldiers so that he could open the door. I looked at the man standing there, but I didn't recognize him.

"Do you know who I am?" he asked

"No, I don't," I replied trying to figure out

"I am Mama's brother," he said.

"No, you're not," I said. "One of Mama's brothers is in the army and the other one is in Burundi, but neither of them has a beard."

The man pulled out a photograph and showed it to me. It was exactly the same photo that my mother had had of one of her brothers – without the beard. It was another emotional reunion.

Uncle Aime had come to take me back with him to Burundi. From there he was planning to send me to my mother's cousin in Gabon, who was willing to adopt me. The Major was away fighting at the time, and I was very reluctant to leave without asking his permission, but my uncle said that we would come back at a later date and speak to him.

Though I was so happy to go with my uncle, I also felt very guilty that I was leaving the house of a man who had loved me as his own child without saying goodbye. Before we left for Burundi, my uncle took me to say goodbye to both my father's cousin and her family and to the woman in Nyanza who had taken care of me in the first weeks after the genocide. My uncle shared the same values as my mother, always reminding me to be thankful and appreciative of those who had been good to me.

To my utter dismay, when we arrived in Burundi, a war had broken out there. I immediately regretted having decided to come back with my uncle. "You have brought me here to die," I said to him. My stay in Burundi was awful. I felt constantly afraid. I could not sleep and, when I did, I had the most terrible nightmares and I would have to go and sleep in my uncle's bed. In the nightmares I was always running, running, running... trying to get away. It was so terrifying that I was afraid to fall asleep. I could not bring myself to tell my uncle any of the details about what had happened – I was not yet ready to talk about it. And I suspected that my uncle was not ready to hear how his sister and her family were murdered.

I stayed with my uncle for three months. He was so kind to me and so patient with a traumatized teenager girl. He would pretend to teach me how to drive a car by letting me release the car hand brake every time we left home and put it back on when we returned. And this alone made me happy. My uncle would tell jokes all the time to make me laugh and try to forget my brokenness and how much I missed my family. He would also introduce me to his friends as his daughter even though he was not yet married. This made me happy. I stayed at his place until he had managed to sort out all the papers that I needed to travel to Gabon.

There was no direct flight to Gabon, so I had to change planes twice. I felt very anxious. For one thing, I had hardly ever seen a plane before, let alone fly on one and, of course, I was already feeling extremely vulnerable. My uncle's friend who was also an extended family member, worked at the airport and she asked one of my fellow passengers who was also Rwandan if he would keep an eye on me. She did not know that this man was himself a Hutu killer fleeing justice in Rwanda. During the flight the man quizzed me about what was going on in Rwanda. He particularly wanted to know whether the situation was now reversed and the Tutsis were killing the Hutus. He also asked me penetrating questions about my family circumstances. I felt very uncomfortable talking to him and said as little as I could. Not wanting him to know that all my family had been killed and I was now on my own, I told him I was on my way to join my family in Gabon.

The first stop was at Douala airport in Cameroon. My uncle had arranged for someone he knew there to look after me until the flight to Gabon was due, but unfortunately this person simply failed to turn up. The Hutu man who was looking after me deposited me in a chair in the airport lounge and went off, purportedly to sort out some papers, but he simply never came back. So I was left waiting and waiting. When I eventually realized he wasn't going to come back, I didn't know what to do. I tried to speak to one of the airport staff, but I couldn't speak French and no one could speak Kinyarwanda.

In the end a policeman managed to find another passenger with the same passport as me, who was able to interpret. They nearly put me on a plane to the Ivory Coast, but just in time I realized that it was the wrong plane, and I kept repeating, "No, no, no...," until they looked at my ticket again and worked out that I was meant to be flying to Gabon. As the flight did not depart until 6.00 the next evening, I spent a whole night and a whole day waiting in the airport. Once at Libreville in Gabon, I had to take another flight to my final destination at Franceville, but since the connecting plane did not leave for two days, I stayed with a friend of the couple who were adopting me. I just slept solidly those two days.

Although I was very grateful to my mother's cousin, Reuben, and his wife, Anne, for adopting me and very appreciative of all they were doing for me, the time I spent in Gabon was extremely tough for me. I felt so alone. There was no one there who could possibly have any understanding of what I had been through, no one I could talk to. As well as the personal trauma I had endured I was coping with deep grief. In addition I was suffering ongoing physical problems as a result of the injuries I had incurred, with the injury to my head causing frequent swelling and painful headaches. I started school about three weeks after arriving in Gabon and had to adapt to learning in a totally new language. But this was easy in comparison with coping with the intense isolation and trauma I felt inside. So many times I would come home from school and lock myself in my room for days and days, crying and crying. I could not sleep. When I did sleep, I would wake up screaming in terror. I felt completely bereft.

Photographs

Pictures of Frida and her family before the Genocide. Frida received these few pictures from friends and relatives that were not in Rwanda during the Genocide as all her family albums were destroyed. Some pictures after the genocide have also been included.

1. Frida's paternal grandparents

2. Frida's parents wedding 1977

3. From the left: Frida's sister Mimi Solange (Twins with Kiki Cesar) aged 12, Frida aged 10, youngest brother Dominique Regis aged 5, House Boy – Mbangukira (photo cut), younger brother Alestude aged 8, oldest Brother – Kiki Cesar (Twins with Mimi Solange) aged 12, and cousin Alain aged 10

4. From the left: Frida's cousin, her brother- Kiki Cesar, paternal Grandparents: Stephane and Margret, younger brother Alestude aged 3, her sister Mimi Solange (Twins with Kiki) age of 7 and Frida at the age of 5

NOTE: Picture damaged because it was found in Frida's aunt Clemence's pocket after she was killed (Clemence's picture on page 110)

5. Frida's older sister Mimi Solange

6. Frida's aunt Clemence (on her dad side)

7. Frida (last on the front row) with cousin Deliphine (1st on the front row) cousin and best friend Adeline who also survived (2nd on the front row) together with friends, were part of a dancing group at the ordination of Frida's uncle into priesthood

8. From left: Frida's cousins Valerie age 7, Clarisse age 8, Frida middle age 7, Clement age 10, and Fils Eric on their 1st communion sharing a drink as the families came together for a combined party

9. From left: Frida's parents, Frida at the age of 7 and her aunt and Godmother Odette on Frida's 1st communion day

10. Frida aged 14, just a few weeks after the genocide. Together with a few relatives, they were given a place to stay in Kimihurura, Kigali

11. Frida with *Nirere Marie,* the lady that saved Frida's life. After hearing Frida's voice crying out while deep in the pit, she ran to tell the young man Lambert who dug Frida out of the ditch where she was buried alive with her family. Nirere has now passed away but left three boys and a daughter behind, plus a couple of grandchildren.

12. Simon, Frida's old neighbor who hid Frida and 8 other members of her family under a small bed for a week. Simon is still alive and has helped Frida in rebuilding her family home.

13. Frida's Dad Bernard Munyabitare, who was a successful businessman

14. Frida's happy days lost. From left: youngest brother Regis at the aged 3, Cesar Kiki her older brother aged 9, younger brother Alestude aged 6, Solange Mimi her older sister and twins with Kiki, aged 9, and Frida in a blue jacket aged 7.

15. Frida on the right at the age of 8, with her friend Joyeuse also aged 8, and her little brother Dieudonne (cut from picture on the left) whose two little brothers, Joyeux aged 5 and Olivier aged 4, were killed with Frida's family. Joyeuse's younger sister Claudette was also Frida's best Friend.

16. Top photo: Frida's home demolished during the Genocide. Bottom photo: Frida later rebuilt the home

17. Victims' remains after the Genocide against the Tutsis in Rwanda

18. Frida's family memorial located at her Grandfather's house

19. Frida, after giving her life to Christ, leading a group of students in prayer at her high school of APE Rugunga

20. Frida's dad was given a decent burial in December 2008 and laid to rest with the rest of his family after a long journey of searching for his bodily remains.

21. Frida in recent times with her three Children: Maxwell now 13, Natasha 12 and Asher Regis soon to be 10

Chapter 8
Christ in Me

In 1995, having returned to Rwanda for a visit, I refused to go back to Gabon. It was just such a relief to meet up with my cousin Adeline and be able to talk with someone who had been through what I had been through. My uncle Aime, who by now had returned from Burundi and was living in Kigali, didn't try to force me to go back. He said there was no point, and anyway my adopted parents were themselves planning to return to Rwanda soon. The decision was made that I would go to boarding school, and I asked to be allowed to return to the one I had attended before the genocide, which another cousin, Karabo, was also attending.

Being back in Rwanda and at the boarding school of my choice did not make life any easier for me. The three girls I shared a room with, including my cousin, were really friendly. Two of them had survived the genocide, and had therefore shared many of the same experiences I had and had suffered greatly. But there was one way in which I felt they could not relate to my experience. They were not alone as I was alone. Both girls still had their mother and step- mother, and my cousin also had her brother and her sisters. I felt so alone. My heart ached with grief.

The intense pain and crippling loneliness were there all the time – during every waking moment, and I was hardly able to sleep. When I went to bed I would fall asleep, only to wake in the middle of the night screaming in terror from my nightmares and then lay awake, crying and crying until my pillow was soaked through with my tears. I constantly had a terrible headache, which meant my schoolwork was suffering, and I was frequently in a bad mood. I felt really, really bad. I did not feel able to talk to anyone about what I was feeling. I cut myself off and withdrew into myself. And it wasn't until later that I understood that it's was a depression that I was dealing with.

And salt was continuously being rubbed into my raw wounds by the fact that on a day-to-day basis I was being forced to interact with Hutus. Most of my teachers were Hutus. My fellow pupils were Hutus. It was as if the genocide had never happened. My thoughts raged and rampaged in my head. How can these Hutus who killed my parents and my brothers and sisters now be teaching me in class? How can I be calmly sitting alongside Hutus as my classmates? These questions tormented me.

To make matters worse some Hutus tried to distance themselves from what had happened by pretending they were Tutsis. One day I was totally and utterly incensed by a conversation one of my room-mates relayed to me. I was getting dressed in my bedroom at the time. One of the Hutu girls, she told me, had actually had the audacity to say that I was really a Hutu. She claimed I was pretending to be Tutsi because my family had been killed when the Tutsis had taken control of the country after the genocide. I was so angry that, without even bothering to finish dressing, I went and found the girl and slapped her across the face.

It had all become too much for me. My head injury flared up again and I was sent to see a doctor at Kigali Hospital for a check-up. As well as giving me some pills for the swelling, the doctor diagnosed that I had malaria and prescribed quinine. All the way back to school in the taxi I was planning how I would use these pills to try commit suicide. I could not go on anymore.

When I got back to school one of my roommates, Huguette, found me crying in the toilet. "Why can't you talk to me, Frida?" she pleaded. "Just tell me what's bothering you."

I replied: "I can't tell you my problems – they're too heavy for you."

The next day I took an overdose. I took the tablets the doctor had given me to ease the swelling in my head, plus the malaria tablets and some aspirin. When my roommates found me, I was foaming at the mouth. "Frida is dying. Frida is dying," they screamed. I was taken to hospital where I remained in a coma for nearly three days.

When I regained consciousness, I was filled with utter despair. I felt so ashamed that I had not succeeded in my attempt to commit suicide. Anger burned within me – anger at the Hutus for destroying my family. I also felt totally insignificant and unloved. Without my family I felt I had lost my identity, my sense of belonging, my reason for living. Without those I loved and I knew had loved me I was nothing. There was no reason to go on living.

I couldn't bear people to know that I had tried to commit suicide – especially my relatives who would have been utterly shocked. So I made up a lie. I tried to make everyone believe that, having forgotten to take my malaria pills in the morning, I doubled the dose at lunchtime. I don't suppose anyone was fooled.

I went back to live with my adopted parents, who by now were also living in Kigali, and for a whole year I sat at home. With nothing else to occupy my thoughts, apart from my daily chores and playing with my adopted parents' two children, I brooded over my sense of isolation, my despair, my anger, my feelings of insignificance. The harrowing sleepless nights continued, wearing me down ever further. Night after night I would cry myself to sleep, only to wake up hours later screaming out, "They're going to kill me! I can see them... I can see them... They're going to kill me!" I was haunted by the images of what I had seen.

As a result of the suicide attempt, my adopted parents and wider family had now begun to realize the extent of the trauma I was suffering. It was arranged that I should attend the Trauma Center, which was a government initiative to help the deeply traumatized survivors of the genocide. It was woefully inadequate in the face of such overwhelming need. Out of all the people I saw at the Center, one young woman particularly stands out in my memory. Her name was Oda. She was only nineteen but she already looked old. She always covered her face with a scarf and she would never talk to anyone. I discovered that the lower part of her face and her shoulder had been obliterated by a gunshot wound. She later went to Europe for reconstruction surgery.

Each Tuesday and Thursday afternoon for two hours I would have an appointment with a psychiatrist and a lady who worked as his assistant or nurse I'm not so sure. She encouraged me to talk about my experiences, asking me such questions as, "How do you feel?" and "What are your dreams for the future?" On many occasions I didn't feel like talking and we all sat in silence.

At the Trauma Center we were each given a book and told to write down our thoughts and feelings in the form of a letter either to God or to someone you had lost. "Insult God, if you want to," they said. "Tell Him how you feel. Express your feelings of anger towards Him." But for me it was a complete waste of time. You could write and write all you wanted – it did not make any difference. In the end I said, "This is rubbish. God is not listening to me. These people are not doing anything to help me." So I stopped going. I probably was wrong as therapy works and helps so many victims.

When the new school year began, I started to attend a local secondary school called APACOPE. By this time I was at least managing to get a bit more sleep. I joined the second year and my studies progressed well. I only had problems when my head injury flared up and terrible headaches stopped me doing my school work. I was in survival mode. But it didn't take much to make me angry, and my fellow students knew that it was best not to mess with me. I could not think about the future, but at least I was managing to make it through each day.

The following school year a new student joined our class. It was now 1998. Her name was Julienne. Like me she was eighteen and was a Tutsi. She had been born in Burundi and her family had not returned to Rwanda until after the genocide. It did not take long for the whole school to find out that Julienne was a born-again Christian and spent every spare moment she had telling her fellow students about Jesus Christ. At that time I hated believers. For me, all Christians were hypocrites and liars. I was frequently getting into heated arguments with the so-called Christians who tried to talk to me about God at school. In the genocide Christians had killed just like everyone else. I had no time for them and I had no time for God, which made my situation worse as running away from God is running away from the peace you need.

When Julienne first started at the school, she didn't know anyone. She would come to school on her own and go home on her own. She came across as a very quiet and serious person, but also quite self-contained. During the breaks she would sit on her own, with her Bible open in front of her, singing about Jesus in a loud, penetrating voice. If she wasn't singing, she would be reading her Bible, almost meditating, and often writing down notes. She came across as a very spiritual person. But whenever she had a chance, Julienne would start talking about Jesus. If she saw a group of students standing together and joking about, she would go over to them and start witnessing to them. Or if a teacher was late turning up to class, she would jump up and use the opportunity to start telling people what faith in God was all about. She really had no conversation apart from talking about God – which, of course, meant that most people avoided her like the plague and went very quiet when she was around.

"Just tell her not to come anywhere near me," I warned my friends. And they knew I was not joking. The previous year there had been another girl in our class who had always been talking about God and we had crossed swords more than once. I had thought she was a Hutu and when she talked about "repenting of my sins," I used to shout at her, "You go and repent yourself – with your family! I haven't got any sins." I would physically push her out of the classroom and on one occasion I threw her Bible out of the window.

I think Julienne must have got the message because she stayed clear of me. There was also an incident in class that must have confirmed to her that I could be quite a stroppy, awkward individual. It happened in an English class. Our English teacher, who was also a journalist and very strict – a very short man – had given the class a text to memorize and everyone was finding it very difficult. As one student struggled to recite the text, someone laughed in the general area of where I was sitting, in a group of six of us, including Julienne. The teacher was very angry. He thought it was me, but I said, "I didn't hear anyone laugh." (At that time I was class captain.) For some reason he completely overreacted and said that he was going to call the parents of the group of six into school, but first he wanted to see our behavior notebooks.

There was a points system in the school for behavior, which was recorded in these notebooks. Anyone going below twenty points landed themselves in serious trouble. He told us he was going to dock ten of our points and call all our parents into school. His talk of our parents made me really angry. I stood up and said, "How dare you talk about my parents! You don't know my parents. You have never met them!" I threw my notebook down in front of him and walked out of the classroom. All the other people in the class were amazed that I could talk like that to a teacher they all feared. I think Julienne was quite shocked too and realized that what she had been told about me was true.

So Julienne steered clear of me and I observed her from a distance. I could not help but be intrigued by her. There was something about her that I could not put my finger on. She seemed very different from the other Christians I had met. She was always singing. She was full of passion. I admired the way she was so bold about her faith, even standing up on buses and in the marketplace in town to tell people about Jesus. But more than anything she seemed at peace. And that was the very thing I was desperate for. Peace. Something to help me make sense of my life. Something to help me understand why I had survived when all the rest of my family were dead.

As a little girl I had had a very strong faith in God. Each morning I had got up early to go to the six o'clock Mass before school and I had loved participating in the worship, either as a server or dancing in our traditional way. I had been deeply impressed and influenced by my grandfather's faith and godly lifestyle. Since the genocide, however, God had seemed a million miles away. I could not understand why He had abandoned my family when we needed Him most. I was confused and very angry.

For the next couple of months I continued to watch Julienne from a distance. Her life was impacting me without her even knowing it. One day I said to my friend Claire, "I am going to get Julienne to talk to me about Jesus, and I am going to become a believer."

"You? become a believer?" she exploded. "If you become a believer, I will too!"

On another occasion I told my friend Kalima that I wasn't interested in any more of his jokes because I was going to become a Christian. "If you become a believer," he teased, "then the whole school will get saved!" They had no idea that I was serious.

I felt I had to talk to Julienne. One morning, during the 10 o'clock break, I went up to her and asked her, "What is it that makes you sing all the time?"

"The peace of Jesus makes me sing," she answered.

"Can that same Jesus give me peace?" I asked.

Although she didn't know anything about me, she replied, "Oh yes, He can."

"Why don't you come and talk to me about Him, then? Why do you talk to other people, and never me?"

"I was planning to," she replied.

"When?" I pressed.

"Maybe later on today."

"Come and talk to me," I insisted. "I want to be a Christian."

Just then, one of my friends who had caught the tail-end of our conversation, interrupted, "She's lying. Don't believe a word of what she says. She hates Christians."

"Keep quiet," I snapped. "It's none of your business."

Later that morning Julienne came over to me and asked me to go with her to a lunchtime fellowship that she attended in the town. "No," I replied immediately. "There are so many killers in those fellowships. I don't want anything to do with them. I just want to become a Christian, find peace and get on with my life. Nothing else." She answered, "Well, there is no way you can grow as a Christian without being part of a fellowship."

Despite my blank refusal, the next day, which was 15

January 1998, before I went to school, I asked my adopted mum whom I later found out was related to Julienne whether it was all right for me to go to the lunchtime fellowship with Julienne. "Yes," she said, "but just this once." So that lunchtime I went with her.

It was held in the Inkurunziza Church in Kigali, which was about two-mile walk from the school. I was amazed to see such a big number of people there. A man called Paul preached and I can remember thinking, "Julienne doesn't know anything about me. How can she have told this preacher all about me?" He preached about the suffering that the Rwandan people had endured, emphasizing that Jesus came to heal the broken-hearted. But out of everything that he said, what really struck me were the words: "Jesus can heal you... Jesus can heal you... Jesus can give you peace..."

When he called for people to come to the front, I rushed forward. He laid his hands on me and prayed for me. I was not alone. Thirty-five others were kneeling at the front with me.

It's hard to explain what happened to me that day, but I felt as though something had left me. I felt a huge sense of relief.

After everyone had been prayed for, we were all taken into a small room and Paul spoke to us. He explained that we were now born again and that our sins were forgiven. We should now begin telling everyone about our new faith and should buy a Bible and start reading it. I thought to myself that I didn't have any money, but I would find some somehow.

I went outside and found Julienne, who was over the moon. We hugged each other and she said, "You're a believer now."

Chapter 9
A Reason to Live Again

From the time Jesus came into my life, I was a different person. I could sleep. I could sing. I could smile. I could begin to relate to people as friends, which I had found so difficult since the genocide. I was happy. Something in me had changed. I had found hope. I felt I could live again.

Within a few months of becoming a Christian the nightmares stopped and I no longer woke up in the night screaming out in terror. I found a Gideon New Testament I had been given at school and read it whenever I could – often when I should have been doing my schoolwork, which I now realize was not very wise. As I began to concentrate on God, attending evening services at my church, reading my bible and prayer instead of my school work. However, I began to understand that there was a reason why I had survived the genocide. God's hand was upon my life and He had saved me for a purpose. I had thought that God had forgotten all about me. Now I began to realize that instead of my life being a big mess, it was a big miracle. My outlook was transformed.

However, from the start being a Christian was not easy. My family, although committed Catholics, in common with many in Rwanda at that time, were deeply suspicious of the new Pentecostal churches and fellowships that were having an impact in the country following the genocide.

When after a very difficult period, they forbade me from attending the lunchtime fellowship at Inkurunziza, I felt I had to take a stand. Becoming a Christian had transformed my life.

Time after time I tried to explain to my relatives the precious peace becoming a Christian had given me and the incredible sense of purpose that was growing within me, but they were not able to understand. Unwilling to jeopardize the progress I had now begun to make in my life, after a family conference at which I was given the ultimatum to choose between church and family, one morning I packed my possessions in one bag and left my adopted parents' home, having no idea where I could go. My uncle Jean who was a Catholic priest then allowed me to live with him for a while but, without any financial support as punishment, life was very difficult.

As I grew older and into a more mature Christian, I now realized how much love my family had for me and that they were concerned about things like school and my future that I did not see as a teenager.

They were concerned I would only focus on being in church and not do my school work, which was true. They were concerned as a loving family that I may only focus on the present and not think of my future career and what would happen to me if I quit school. They were also concerned that I may even just meet a guy in church and marry him before completing my education, and they were very right because that's exactly what happened.

Today I wish I had kept my passion for God burning but also saved the relationship with my family as they still loved and never stopped loving me even when I left them. In my school then there were so many other kids whose relationships with their families suffered because of their faith and because attending a different church than what their families were used to in Rwanda. I always hoped it was different and that our faith did not separate us from those who loved and taken us in after losing our families, but I also understood that following Christ had a price on it. Growing in my new-found faith had become a matter of life or death to me and some of my other friends too. I could not stop then and had no ability to make my family understand, but I thank God that now they do and respect that I'm still growing and pursuing the path of wanting to know the purposes of God in my life.

It was during this difficult time that I started attending Julienne's church, which was called Rwanda for Jesus Church. I simply responded to a suggestion she made that I could come and see what it was like. The first time I went I did not see the Senior Pastor, whom Julienne had told me so much about, as he was preaching at a church in Butare, a two-hour drive away. His brother was preaching that Sunday. I sat at the back, so that I could watch what was going on. I liked the church. At one point in the service, people started talking in a different language but, knowing the pastor had grown up in Uganda, I thought they must be speaking in Luganda. I didn't realize that they were speaking in languages given to them by the Holy Spirit. The following Sunday I returned to Rwanda for Jesus Church and made the decision to make it my church. Not long after I joined the worship team and threw myself into the life of the church.

After a couple of months I began to realize that, although God had provided me with a wonderful church family, I could not cope with the present situation much longer. Having no money to take the bus, the eight-mile walk to school and back each day was taking its toll and my studies were suffering. Occasionally Christians from Inkurunziza or church, knowing my circumstances, would give me money to catch the bus home, but most days I had to walk – and on an empty stomach too, as I had no money to buy lunch. The end of the school year was approaching and I decided that, even though it would be a wrench to leave Julienne and the church, it would be better if the following school year I went back to boarding school. But I was determined to find a school where I would be free to pray and worship and to speak openly about my faith.

My cousin Adeline was at a boarding school in Nyanza called ESPANYA, which stood for Ecole Sécondaire des Parents de Nyanza. She told me that there were a lot of believers at the school and encouraged me to join her there. When I went to the school with my cousin to ask if there was a place available in Senior 4, I was really surprised to find that the administrator of the school was Musoni, the man who had helped me at the end of the genocide and had found a home for me to stay in. He was very happy to give me a place at the school, and this seemed to confirm that it was the right step for me. Julienne was heartbroken when I told her about my decision. By this time we had developed a really close friendship and we both found it hard to say goodbye.

Term started a month later. There was just enough income from renting out my father's house in Kigali to pay for the school fees and to buy my school uniform and equipment. As I started yet another school I had two specific goals in mind: the first to serve God with all my heart and, the second, to study hard and pass all my exams with good grades. By this time I was starting to learn that as a student the only way to show others that you honor God was by doing your job as a student.

By the end of my first week at the school, however, I was feeling rather depressed and deflated by the group of Christians I had met there. They insisted that you couldn't be a Christian if you wore trousers or ear-rings, and they said that women should cover their heads in church. The Christian faith I had embraced had brought me life and freedom. I could not understand their legalism, and I didn't want anything to do with it. About the third week of term I was just coming out of the school shop, where I had bought an avocado to add to the awful-tasting beans and rice we were served for lunch every single day, when I saw someone I recognized entering the school. It was Julienne's brother and he was carrying a huge bag. When I saw the person following in behind him, I just couldn't believe my eyes. It was Julienne! I ran up to her and gave her a big hug. I was so surprised and excited to see her. "What are you doing here?" I asked her. Julienne herself was rather dazed and confused. That morning when she had woken up, she had had no idea that she would be changing schools that day. On her way back from morning prayers at Rwanda for Jesus Church, her brothers had bundled her into a car and brought her to the school. Their aim was to stop Julienne's evangelistic activities, but nothing could stop her.

Julienne had never been to boarding school before so I helped her settle in and showed her the ropes. Since there were not enough beds at the school everyone had to share. I shared with my cousin Adeline. I was really glad that Julienne was able to share with a lovely fellow believer called Jennifer. Julienne and I were both convinced that God had a reason for bringing us back together and was going to do something very exciting at the school.

The very first evening Julienne came to the school we were all in our huge dormitory just getting ready to go to bed when I heard someone trying to gain everyone's attention. That was quite common as there were often announcements that had to be made, so I turned to look. I will never forget what I saw. The person trying to attract everyone's attention was Julienne and she was standing on top of one of the bunk beds that filled the room. In true African style the enormous room was jam-packed with bunk-beds leaving only a tiny passageway between for the girls to squeeze through.

She shouted out, "I want to tell you all about Jesus who is willing to save anyone who will come to Him." She then proceeded to tell the 300 girls in the dormitory that they needed to receive Jesus as their Lord and Savior. At the end she asked everyone to close their eyes while she prayed. Although rather bemused, everyone respected her request. That evening six girls gave their lives to Christ and many others were interested. They just couldn't believe that someone so new to the school could have the courage to do what she had just done. It was an unforgettable experience. By the time Julienne had been at the school a week, everyone knew her.

All the Christians in the school were encouraged by Julienne's bold stand and the Christian group had an influx of members. A couple of weeks later, two of the girls who went to Kigali Restoration Church when they were at home told us that the church was holding a forty-day fast, and we decided to join them "in the spirit." Each morning we woke up early and had a time of prayer at 3.00 a.m. – it was my job to creep around all the beds in the dark waking everyone up. We then fasted until 6.00 p.m. each evening, also meeting to pray and read the Bible each lunchtime and evening. We broke our fast with a meal of rice mixed with black beans in water and had mild black tea without sugar. It did not taste very good, but it kept us going. Fasting was a radical new idea for the Church in Rwanda or at least to my knowledge at that time and, to tell the truth, we didn't know much about it. We even thought it was wrong to swallow any water when we were brushing our teeth! By the end of our fast we had seen miracles of people coming to Christ both inside and outside of the school.

Trouble was brewing, however. Some of the girls fell sick and the headmaster discovered that it was because they had been fasting. One girl had to be sent home because she became so ill, and her parents came to the school to complain. Julienne, as the leader of the group, was summoned to the headmaster's office and she was told that the fasting must stop. When she said that she was not prepared to stop it, she was suspended and sent home while the situation was dealt with. Before she left, Julienne told me to lead the group in her absence and to be honest I was so scared that I would be next to be sent home, but I refused to show my fear to the girls.

The following Sunday Julienne was due to preach at a local church in Nyanza, Eglise Presbytérienne au Rwanda, which was the church we used to attend each Sunday. When the pastor came to the school to talk to Julienne about it and discovered that she was not there, he asked to speak to me and invited me to preach instead. I told him that I had never preached before, but he seemed convinced I could do it and eventually I agreed. It was a huge challenge for me to stand up in front of a congregation of over a hundred people and the elders of the church and I was terrified.

Sitting at the front of the church alongside the pastor, I kept my eyes firmly shut until the time for me to preach came. As I stood up everyone cheered and clapped their hands. Sweating and shaking with fear I preached for the next forty-five minutes, speaking about what had happened to me and about God's power to change lives. At the end I asked people to come forward if they wanted to give their life to Jesus, and nearly the whole congregation came and knelt at the front, crying out to God and repenting of their sins. It was amazing. It showed me what God can do, when we trust in Him and not in ourselves. From that day I began to feel and understand a call and the purpose for my miraculous survival. I knew I had to start sharing my story and preach to the world what the Lord had done for me.

After a few days Julienne returned to the school accompanied by her sister. When the headmaster explained the problems Julienne had been causing, her sister confessed that the reason the family had sent her to boarding school was because they could not control her and because she was causing similar problems at her previous school with her preaching activities. Warning Julienne that if she was expelled, her parents would not pay school fees for her at another school, she begged the headmaster to give her sister another chance. Julienne insisted that she could not stop herself talking about Jesus, because it was her life.

Stipulating that the younger girls must stop fasting, the headmaster eventually agreed that the students would be allowed to pray at certain allotted times – but not very early in the morning. Julienne was accepted back into the school. I think that, in fact, the headmaster had noticed that the fasting had had a positive impact on the school and seen that the behavior of many of the most difficult pupils had improved. Even in the town, people were talking about how the school had changed.

Knowing that we had to curb our activities within the school, Julienne came up with a new plan. Each Sunday, which was our only free day, she would take us out into the town to preach in the market-place after church. One person would preach and then the rest of us would talk to anyone who was interested. As a group of girls working together we were often the butt of jokes and a great deal of teasing from the lads who worked on the stalls, but it was worth it to see people coming to Jesus. This was also the same market where my father had some of his business before the Genocide. So a few people in town knew who I was and I knew that word would get to my family soon.

Later on, we started going to the hospital, where we would do washing for the patients, many of whom had been abandoned by their families. Working alongside Julienne, I began to grow in confidence. I had caught her passion to spread the gospel and I never wanted to lose it.

Chapter 10
Too Evil to Forgive

I was growing as a Christian and becoming passionate about God, but there was one topic I did not like to hear preachers talk about. I used to shut my ears whenever it came up. It was the topic of forgiveness. Sometimes preachers from Uganda and the West, knowing what the Rwandan people had been through, would come to the lunchtime fellowship and speak very strongly about the need for us to forgive. But I used to say to myself, "These people can only talk about forgiveness because they have no idea what we have been through."

The examples the preachers used to give of situations where they were required to forgive someone seemed so trivial – even laughable – compared to what had happened to me. An argument with their wife, a misunderstanding between friends, a broken promise, even the betrayal of infidelity in marriage: all these paled in comparison when I considered what I had to forgive. What right did they have to lecture me on the subject? So I closed my ears to the preachers who spoke on forgiveness, as well as my eyes to the Bible verses which challenged me. No way, God, no way! I had every reason not to forgive. Yet now as a grown woman and more mature in the Lord I learnt that this was another kind of pride.

Despising what someone else has been through and

has had to forgive –because of your own pain that you think is deeper or stronger – is a pride, and this pride does not do anything else but stop you from moving towards the grace to forgive and moving forward in God. I also learnt later that this can be a weapon and trick used by Satan to blind you with your own pain.

While nothing could take away the peace and joy I had found when I had met Jesus on that day back in January, my day-to-day life was hard. The loss of my family had left a gaping hole, the pain of which I felt every day. I thought that there was no one who really cared whether I lived or died; no one to share with me the ups and downs of daily living. I was simply an orphan totally alone in the world. Nothing was ever going to change that. Nobody could ever give me back what I had lost and this sometimes led to feelings of self-pity.

And if the constant daily ache in my own heart was not enough, I was living in a country still reeling from the catastrophic events that had taken place. On the one hand, deeply traumatized people who could barely make it through to the end of each day surrounded me. On the other hand were people who were doing their best to pretend that the genocide had never happened or at least that they had had no part in it. People were living side by side with the killers who had destroyed their lives. For all intents and purposes they were getting away with it.

The sense of purpose and destiny that God had

given me for my life was providing me with the strength to go forward. I was focused and determined. Whenever the disturbing topic of forgiveness came up, I would say, "God, I will do whatever you want me to do. I will go and preach the gospel in the villages. I will fast. I am prepared to be persecuted for your name's sake. I will do anything. But I will never forgive the people who destroyed my family." When I think back about this kind of thinking, I realized that I was actually not even obedient to God to do those things without taking care of my own hardened heart and refusing to forgive others yet asking God to forgive me for my own brokenness and sins.

Forgiveness was simply a subject that would not go away. Every time I went to church I was worshiping alongside Hutus and I could not stop the anger and bitterness I felt in my heart from rising. It seemed that so often when I sat down and read the Bible, a verse about forgiveness would spring off the page or when I heard a sermon it was the words "You need to forgive" that sounded louder than all the others. The challenge of forgiveness came to me over and over again.

Everything within me screamed out at the very idea of what God was asking me to do. It made me feel almost physically sick. It was not to be countenanced, not even to be entertained. What those men had done to my family and to me was too evil to forgive. I could never forgive them for murdering my family in front of my eyes. If it had not been for

God's miraculous intervention I would be dead too. They had ripped my life apart and savagely destroyed everything.

And if that evil were not terrible enough, I knew that others had suffered just as much horror and some even worse. I had heard of people herded into churches and massacred. I had heard of pregnant women who, moments after giving birth, had watched their innocent newborn babies being slaughtered and then been brutally raped by the murderer. I had heard of men deliberately infecting women with AIDS. I had heard of young women gang-raped until they dropped down dead; of tiny, innocent babies being thrown against walls to kill them. No, these horrors were too great. They could never be forgiven. These killers must be punished. They must be made to pay for what they had done.

Whenever the subject of forgiveness came up, I would be thrown into turmoil and become angry, and bitter thoughts would crowd into my mind. But, despite my stubborn refusal to listen, nothing would make God's quiet but insistent voice go away. My argument with God would run along these lines: "Lord, why do you keep talking to me about forgiveness when I am not ready to forgive? How can I even begin to forgive people for what they have done without them even coming to me and asking for that forgiveness? I wouldn't know where to start. Yes, I can forgive the girl at school for telling lies about my family. Yes, I can forgive somebody who has insulted me. Yes, I can forgive a family member for beating me unfairly. Yes, I can forgive those who laugh at me for being a Christian. But how can I ever forgive those brutal murderers who destroyed everything I loved – my parents, my brothers and sisters, my grandparents, my home? Who never showed any mercy but wanted to wipe my tribe off the face of the earth? Who took everything I had so I am left with nothing? How, Lord? No, you are asking too much. I can't go to these people and tell them I forgive them for what they have done."

Part of me was convinced that forgiving these people would help me heal and make my life easier. But I also knew that when my family, friends and fellow survivors learned of my forgiveness they would definitely think I had gone insane. I worried that my forgiveness would be considered a betrayal and an insult to my fellow survivors who were then – and even today – still hurting. I also understood that my forgiveness would not just be a gift to those who had not asked for it or would ever deserve it, but a gift to my hurting self.

But God would not give up. Again and again He placed the challenge of forgiveness before me. "Will you forgive as I forgive?" "No, God," I persisted. "You cannot ask this of me. Haven't I been through enough? You can send me to the farthest corner of the globe and I will willingly go, but you cannot ask me to forgive the Hutus who destroyed my life and everything I loved."

The debate within me raged on over months and God

did not let it drop. I read Jesus' parable about a king who wrote off the huge debts of one of his servants but was extremely angry when the forgiven man would not show the same mercy to a fellow servant, who by comparison owed him a very small sum. In the story the king turned the man over to the jailers to be imprisoned and tortured until he paid back all he owed, saying in conclusion, "This is how my heavenly Father will treat each of you unless you forgive your brother from your heart" (Matthew 18:35). I tried to reason that He couldn't possibly be speaking about such enormous crimes as murder and genocide. Surely God made allowances for people like me who had suffered such great loss?

I went back to this passage again and again, trying to come to terms with the huge challenge it presented. As I did, God began to show me that masked behind the immense sense of injustice I felt was another much less noble emotion: self-pity. I wanted the world to look at me and say, "Poor Frida. Look what she has suffered." I was cradling my loss as a comfort blanket. I wanted people to feel sorry for me. But God showed me that no child of His ever needed to be pitied. I began to understand that self-pity was a monster that would devour me if I continued to give in to it. I did not want to remain resentful or grow into a bitter old lady. Instead, I wanted to become a better woman each day and realized that if I really meant this I needed to do the hard work it required.

Yet I also felt that if I did forgive, it would be like letting the killers go free and unpunished. No punishment could ever repay what we survivors lost in the genocide. We lost more than just our loving families. We have to live with and deal with depression, anxiety and fear for the rest their lives. Is there an equal punishment for someone who has caused you so much pain? Is there an equal punishment for someone who has given you such a terrible burden to carry each day? Not wanting to be the judge of such evil acts, I was learning to let God be God. I was learning to allow him to vindicate and advocate for me.

Once I was willing to face up to the self-pity in my heart, to ask God for His forgiveness and allow the Holy Spirit to change my attitude, I was able to move on in my thinking about forgiveness. From a blank refusal even to contemplate making such a step, I began to consider what the consequences might be if I refused to obey God. Just suppose I refused to forgive the killers of my family. What would be the result in my own life and how would it affect my service to God? God, I knew, would never allow me to be a preacher of His love if my heart remained unforgiving. Refusing to forgive would staunch the flow of God's love in my own life. Bitterness and resentment would take over and work like a cancer to destroy me. I imagined myself becoming old well before my years and people pointing the finger as I went about my life, saying, "She's the one who survived the genocide, but her life finished when she refused to forgive those who wiped out her family." Later I understood that forgiveness is an act of courage rather than a weakness in one's life.

One thing I was sure about was that God had not saved my life from the grave so that I could struggle on through the rest of my life, withered up inside. He wanted to use me as someone through whom His love could flow and be an inspiration to others to get hold of His love. Yet still, as I argued back and forth, the mountain that God was placing before me, seemed too immense, too arduous, and insurmountable.

I did not speak to anyone about the challenge I was being given by God. I prayed about it continually and I also spent days fasting, asking God to help me to do what He was asking me to do. So desperate was I to find a breakthrough in this area of my life that each Friday I prayed through the night, pleading with God to guide me and help me.

Time and time again as I wrestled with the subject of forgiveness, I came back to two key passages in the Bible. The first was Luke 23:34 where, as Jesus is dying on the cross, He cries out, "Father, forgive them, for they do not know what they are doing." I began to realize that, like my family, Jesus had been hounded and hated to the point where members of His own people and those he had come to save had murdered him. He had been persecuted as we had been persecuted. He had been tortured and abused as we had been. And, in the end, He had been murdered as my family had been. There was great comfort for me in knowing that God's own Son had suffered in the way that I had suffered, but for a long time I could not get any further. "Yes," I reasoned, "but Jesus was God. As God He could forgive His murderers, but I am a human being and not God."

It was many months of agonizing before the breakthrough came, and I understood for the very first time that, yes, the Jesus who was nailed to the cross was one hundred percent God, but He was also one hundred percent man. When the nails were driven through His hands and He was hung on a cross, He had a human body just like me, He felt the pain as I did, and yet He could still say, "Father, forgive them..."

The second key passage was Acts 7, which records how one of the first believers, Stephen, was stoned to death for his faith in Jesus – the first Christian martyr. Like Jesus, in the midst of his suffering and pain, Stephen was able to forgive those who were killing him. As he lay dying, he cried out, "Lord, do not hold this sin against them." Stephen was a human being just like me. He had no greater resources than I had to enable him to forgive his murderers. God the Holy Spirit had enabled him to forgive. I understood that if Stephen could forgive, then I could too. As I allowed this insight to change my thinking and soften my heart, I began to put myself in the place of Stephen and imagine myself saying, "Lord, do not hold this sin against them," as he did when the stones were being hurled against his body.

As the Holy Spirit revealed more and more to me, I began to understand that at the time of the genocide the devil had taken over my country and there was a spirit behind the people who had perpetrated these terrible crimes. It was the devil who had driven the Hutus to fulfill their stated aim of exterminating every single Tutsi. There was no other way to explain the speed in which the bloodlust had swept through the country, or the depths of depravity to which the killers had sunk. Certainly the Hutus were responsible for their own actions but there was no other way to explain why they had torn babies out of the womb, or why they had put tiny babies inside cooking pots and smashed them to death. They had committed unspeakable crimes of brutality against women; they had buried people alive. These killers had decorated their bodies with their victims' limbs and had drunk human blood. Justice had to take place but even more heavenly justice needed to intervene for a survivor like me to be able to live with these horrific memories. And by this I mean I needed to let God be God. I needed to let him be the judge as I watched him deliver me from the spirit of bitterness and anger for what had happened to my people and me.

Although many of the killers were high on alcohol and drugs, I knew that something must have overtaken them to sink to those levels of depravity. Even Hutus living in the most remote areas of the country, who had no access to the radio stations pumping out their poisonous message of hate and destruction, had joined in perpetrating these atrocious acts. The only explanation could be that an utterly evil power had compelled them. Yes, the hatred that was planted in their minds by their own government had started showing its fruits. As Jesus had died on the cross, He had cried out, "Father, forgive them, for *they do not know* what they are doing," and I began to understand that the Hutus, too, had not known what they were doing. Although this in no way absolves them from their individual and collective responsibilities for their crimes, I knew they were swept up into something that was beyond their control. I recognized too, that this kind of mentality or understanding could make a survivor even bitterer. But my aim was to take my power back from my enemy. Had I let myself continue to grow bitter, perhaps I would not have made it as far as I have. Or perhaps I would be alive but suffering even more than I was before receiving Christ.

I also considered the shameful truth that many who claimed to be Christians had participated and even taken the lead in the killings – even reading from the Bible to justify the acts they were about to commit. I then realized that it is not those who say they are Christians who are Jesus' true followers but those who do what He commands. Jesus was asking me to forgive my enemies. If I wanted to be His disciple there could be no doubt about what I should do. I began to realize that I could not go on being part of the worship group at church and taking part in other church activities if I was not willing to forgive. I would be a hypocrite – the very thing in my mind I was often accusing Hutu Christians of being.

Very gradually, over a period of months, God brought me to the point where I was able to say, "Lord, I *want* to forgive." This was a momentous step forward, but I still felt overwhelmed by the sense that it was totally beyond my capacity to do so. I did not have the resources inside me; I did not know where to begin. My cry was, "Lord, I want to be like you. I want to put my feet into your footprints. I want to obey you, but I can't in my own strength. In my strength, I can't forgive the people who have destroyed my life. But I know I am your child, and I ask you to give me a new heart and the courage to follow your example." This kind of surrendering and prayer was heartfelt and the Lord saw my willingness to follow him and his example. I recognized I did not have what it took and had nothing left in me to help myself but wanted to trust him alone that he had me in his hands.

Two months later I felt the Lord God had answered my prayer. Perhaps the final stepping stone in this long and harrowing process had been the realization that both Jesus and His disciple Stephen had not waited for their enemies to come to them to ask for forgiveness, but had taken the initiative in forgiving those who were about to take their lives away from them. I realized that God was asking me to take the first step by going and telling my family's murderers that I forgave them. I needed to step out in faith, believing that He would do the rest.

I decided to begin with the man who had killed my father. I asked my cousin Emmanuel, who was not a believer, to go with me to the prison in a village near our family home, where I knew he and some of the other men who had killed people in the genocide were being held.

"I've heard that you have become a Christian," Emmanuel said. "What are you planning to do at the prison?"

"I just wanted to see the killers, that's all." I was deliberately vague.

When we arrived at the prison, we asked one of the warders on duty whether we would be allowed to see François, my father's killer. He said we could, but explained that François was on a labor gang building some new houses a short distance away from the prison and would need to be fetched – it wouldn't take long. As we stood waiting, I caught sight of some of my former neighbors among the prison inmates and was suddenly gripped with an awful fear. "What am I doing here?" I asked myself. "Am I doing the right thing? What am I going to say to him?" As the prison warder returned bringing François, the fear intensified and I felt absolutely terrified. "What if he has got some kind of weapon in his pocket?" I whispered to my cousin.

"Don't be afraid," he reassured me. "He is powerless

now."

François stood in front of me, arms folded and leaning back on one foot, a dismissive sneer spread right across his face, as if to say, "What do you want?" I wanted to reach out and shake his hand, but I was suddenly overwhelmed by an uncontrollable emotion. I burst into tears and dropped down on the ground, curling myself up into a little ball with my arms covering my head.

"What's happening to you? What's happening to you?" my cousin asked.

"Take me home," I sobbed. I needed to get out of there.

I was not ready. The sight of the man who in cold blood had murdered my father had opened the floodgate of all the raw emotions that were still locked up so tightly inside me. I had thought I was ready, but when the moment came I could not go through with it. I cried all the way home in the bus. Later that night and in the days that followed, I wept before God and cried out, "God, why are you torturing me like this? Can't you see now that I can't do it? You know I want to, but I can't. I will only be able to do it if you give me your heart."

A year later, and after much more prayer, I felt ready to make a second attempt to forgive. First, I went to try and see John, the man who had nearly killed me. I discovered that a bomb had killed him while he was fleeing to the Congo. So I went to visit his sister instead. I told her that I had forgiven John and had released him from what he had done. On hearing my words, she cried.

Then I went back to the neighborhood where I had grown up and went from door to door telling everyone that I had found Jesus. I wanted them to know that I had forgiven them. On hearing my words, several people gave their lives to Jesus.

Perhaps the most poignant encounter was with an old neighbor called Elina, whose daughter had occasionally come to do her family's washing at the standpipe with me. Elina and her family members were Seventh Day Adventists. Like John, Elina's husband Jason had also been killed while fleeing to the Congo. As I sat in her home explaining why I had come, I could see cupboards that had been taken from our home filled with our old plates, cups and glasses. Elina and her children were even wearing our old clothes. At this point I wanted to ask "for real people?" "Not only did you kill my family but you even have the guts to talk to me while wearing my clothes?" But I knew it was not going to help me accomplish my mission if I said something about it. Thirsty from speaking, I asked her for a glass of water and, as she brought it to me, there was a flash of recognition that she was about to hand me my own glass and she hesitated, very embarrassed. I quickly said, "I have not come to take anything from you. I have come to make peace with you." I drank the water and prayed for her family. My neighbor just shook her head and opened her mouth as if to speak, but she could not find any words. Shortly afterwards I left her home with the words, "Peace be with you."

As I made my way home on the bus this time I was rejoicing. I was so grateful to God that He had given me the courage to do what I had done and that some people had even turned to Him. At the same time, however, I was very aware of how these people were suffering. In their eyes I could see their fear that I had come to take my revenge. I could also see very clearly that they were not at peace. Not only that, but they were struggling to make ends meet and were becoming poorer and poorer. Where previously they had worked for people like my father, the employment situation now was very difficult and many people had no work. This understanding fueled my prayers and now I was truly able to say from my heart, "Father, forgive them for they did not know what they were doing."

In time I was able to return to the prison to deliver my message of forgiveness to François, who told me the whole story of what had happened. It seems that when the killers had finished with my family, Papa could stand it no longer. He came down from his hiding place and gave himself up to them. Papa was forced to dig his own grave and told to wait by it while the killers went off to have their lunch. Upon returning, they found him waiting – I believe that, having seen his whole family murdered, death had overwhelmed him. Papa asked for time to pray and just as he said "Amen," François killed him. An eyewitness has since told me that my father was forced to remove the dungarees and socks he was wearing before he was killed. François took these, and Papa was therefore murdered and buried naked.

I asked François where my father's grave was but he said he could not remember. When I pressed him, he told me a place but when we dug there, we could not find anything. Not long afterwards François and many like him were released from prison. If people confess what they have done, they are set free but did the community work to rebuild what they had destroyed.

I began the process of forgiveness because I understood that this was what Jesus was asking me to do. What I discovered was that, as I did so, forgiveness brought me great healing. On becoming a Christian, I had found new peace, but this peace increased immeasurably as I forgave the people who had destroyed my life.

I once met a Hutu man who had become a Christian while in prison, after having been sentenced for his part in the atrocities. As we talked together, I asked him what had pushed him as a Hutu to do what he had done. He told me that they had acted under pressure from the government.

"What if the Hutus were in the same position again?" I asked. "Would you do the same thing again?"

"No," he answered. "Having seen what I have seen, I could never do the same thing again."

Our conversation moved on to the subject of forgiveness. I asked him if he had ever gone to the families of those he had killed to ask for their forgiveness. He replied that he had confessed his sins to God, and that was enough: he did not need to ask for forgiveness from anyone else. Taking his hands in mine I said, "You should go and ask for forgiveness from the people you have harmed and make peace with them. Otherwise blood will always be on your hands. There are so many people who are still crying because of what they have suffered at your hand. You need to go to them and ask them to forgive you."

"No," he said, "God has forgiven me, and that is enough. I know you will never forgive me."

"I have forgiven you," I said. Once we understand that you do not only sin against God but against his people too then we have truly understood what forgiveness is all about. But you can't just say that God forgave me and that is enough when you know that you have damaged people's lives.

As I set out on the pathway of forgiveness and saw first-hand the great pain that was in my nation as a result of the genocide, God began to give me a vision to help the broken-hearted people of Rwanda to find healing. I had the idea that, instead of celebrating my twentieth birthday on 14 March (the day I was born), I would celebrate it on 15 January, the day I had become a Christian two years before and I would tell my friends about the vision God was giving me to help those who were still in deep pain. On my birthday cake were written the words "God heals the broken-hearted."

When the time came to eat the cake, I made a short speech to my friends, including my pastor.

"The reason that the words 'God heals the broken-hearted' are on this cake and not 'Happy Birthday' is because today I am celebrating the fact that God has healed my heart. God has given me a vision to help other people. I know that one day the Lord will make a way for me to have full knowledge of how to help the hurting and traumatized people, as well as the orphans and other people who have gone through so much. When I was born, my parents gave me the name Umuhoza, which means 'counselor' or 'comforter.' I believe that, although they did not know it at the time, it was a prophetic name. I want to do what this name means: I want God to give me a heart to comfort people who are really suffering and show them that God can heal their broken hearts using my story".

Chapter 11
The Courage To Live Again

It has been twenty-three years now since the genocide took place, but the memories of our loved ones will never be forgotten. My traumatic memories now have no power over me. That is not to say that I do not still feel the acute loss of my family, but the past no longer holds me back. Although my enemies chose me to die, I know that God destined me to live. I know that there was a very special reason why I lived and fifteen other members of my family died. I am determined to fulfill the destiny that God has for my life. Indeed, some of that destiny I have already fulfilled, but I know there is more to come – much more!

When I returned home from Gabon as a sixteen- year-old, I was heartbroken to discover that in my absence my extended family had exhumed the bodies of my family and reburied them in a communal grave next to my grandfather's house. The grave contains fifteen bodies – it should have contained sixteen. I know that the reason that my extended family chose to do it in my absence was to spare me further pain, but unwittingly this robbed me of an appropriate and necessary part of the grieving process. To tell the truth, not being there on that occasion broke my heart even more. I am, however, extremely grateful that my beloved family is buried together in a place where they will always be remembered. In fact, just across the track from the grave, there is a mass grave containing the remains of 1200 Tutsis, which is in the process of being made into a public memorial site for the citizens of Nyanza.

The authorities chose to position it near my grandfather's house because he was such a respected and revered member of the community. And the community has memorial services known as "Kwibuka" which means "To Remember" every year during the same period of when the genocide happened. When the rest of my family was given a decent burial, there was a very important part of that family missing and that was my own father's body. I, however, never stopped looking and searching for his body. My main hope in locating where his body was, lied with his killer; François. But since that day when I visited him in prison to tell him I had forgiven him, on which occasion he freely admitted to having murdered my father, François changed his tune.

As soon as I heard that François had been released from prison, I felt compelled to go and see him again. My only reason for going was to beg him to tell me where my father's body is buried. It was September 27, 2006 and, even though it was raining that day, I still decided to go because I was desperate to hear what he had to say. I really wanted to get to the truth.

My cousin Blaise came with me, and we stood and talked on the doorstep of François' house in the rain. To Blaise's and my surprise François recognized my cousin but not me. As before, his attitude was hostile and defensive. He seemed to be looking down his nose at me as if to say, "What do you want?"

"Don't you know who this is?" Blaise asked. When it was clear that François didn't, Blaise continued, "Please try and remember your former neighbors – she is one of their daughters. Surely you can remember?"

Seeing that Blaise was beginning to get upset, I broke in and said, "I know it's been awhile since you saw me, but I am Frida, Bernard's daughter. I have come to ask you some important things that I want to know about my father."

Before I had even finished my sentence, François said aggressively, "And do you think I know? I don't know anything about your father at all... at all."

When he said that, I was really taken aback. By this point in the conversation, it had begun to rain much harder and his wife and children, who were just returning to the house, urged us to come inside, but we stayed where we were. Feeling desperate to get hold of the one piece of information I had come to discover, I pressed François, saying: "Please. You're the one who told me that you had killed my father when I came to see you in 1999. Now you're denying it, but that's OK. At least, if you know where the body is, please show me. I have not come to judge you, but to ask you please to help me."

"OK," he replied. "If that's all you want, let's go. I'm

sure that his body was taken to be buried with the rest of your family but, anyway, let's go."

When we reached the stretch of road where the roadblock had been set up during the genocide and used as a killing center, François stopped. "This is the place," he said. "Bernard came up from his father's house and found me sitting here by the roadblock. He looked terrified. He wasn't wearing shoes, but was just in his socks. He told me that he wanted to die because he had just seen his wife and children being killed and he couldn't face going on living. I told him to leave but he wouldn't listen to me. In fact, he seemed very confused. He asked me to kill him, but I insisted that I couldn't do such a thing. So, he said he was going to wait for the killers to come back from his father's home, knowing that they would kill him. I begged him to leave but he wouldn't. Instead he sat down with his head between his knees and just waited. He was breathing very fast."

After a pause, he continued, "Not long afterwards the killers who'd gone to your grandfather's house came back and found him there. They asked me what he was doing there, but I told them that he was a brother and they should leave him alone. They ordered me to kill him; I refused. Just then your father said that he had some beers that he'd been keeping at Kabayiza's house since before all the killing had started and that he wanted us all to have a drink on him. We all went to Kabayiza's house. When we got there, your father told Kabayiza to bring the beer and he did. While we were drinking together, your father told us that he'd given a cow to Kabayiza and that no one should take it away from him.

"Before we'd finished drinking the beers, some more of the killers who'd been at your grandfather's house came and discovered us all there. When they found your father and me sitting side by side, they were furious. 'How dare you sit there with that cockroach we've been trying to find for a month now?' they shouted. I told them that he wasn't a cockroach but a brother, but they wouldn't listen. They told him to stand up and then they pushed him out telling him to go with them. Then we all came back here. When we got here, your father begged us to give him just a few minutes to pray, which they did and while he was praying, I stepped back."

"What did he say in his prayer?" I asked.

"I told you I stepped back because I didn't want to see him being killed, therefore I couldn't hear his prayer, but I did hear him say 'Amen' and, as soon as he said it, he was hit on the back of his head with a big stick. He didn't scream – he just died there and then."

"Who hit him?" I demanded to know. "Because if you were standing nearby, you know at least who did it, don't you?"

"Karori hit him," he replied.

By then I was so upset that I felt like crying, but I swallowed my tears because I didn't want him to see me crying and stop telling me his story or even give him that pleasure of seeing my brokenness. As he spoke, I was filming him and recording his voice using my mobile phone.

"I swear I didn't kill your father," François continued, "even if I confessed it in prison. I saw him being killed, but I didn't touch him."

"Are you sure you didn't do anything to my father?" I pressed. "That you just looked on while he was being killed? Why didn't you do something then?"

"Because I would have been putting my life at risk too. I'd tried to persuade him to get out of there and he refused – what else could I have done?" he said.

"Are you very sure that it was all done here?" I asked.

"Yes, I'm very sure. The reason I know that his body was buried with the others is because people told me," he added.

"How do you know?" Blaise interrupted angrily. "Now that you've told us what you know, just leave it to us and we'll do the rest." Trying to calm him down, I put my hand on his shoulder and said, "Blaise, it's OK. There's no need to be angry. What was done was done. Let's go now. I've seen the place and that's all I wanted. Let's go." Then, turning to François I took my farewell, saying, "Thank you very much for your time and for bearing with me in the rain. Please feel free to get in touch with me any time and tell me anything else that you remember. You can always tell my cousin Emmanuel who lives in this area and I can come back any time you want to talk to me. I want you to know that I have forgiven all of you with all my heart." As hard as this was I had such huge desire to have a closure about my father's death and take that honor to at least give him a decent burial; since I had missed out on everyone else.

At that he just said, "No, there's nothing else to add to what I've told you. I've told you everything I know. Don't ask me ever again. I'm innocent. If I'd done it, I would have told you, and that's that."

After thanking him again, we took our leave.

I left feeling extremely upset that this man had changed his story. When I got home that evening, exhausted, I knew François was lying to me because there were eyewitness accounts of him murdering my father. I decided to return to Nyanza the following Wednesday when François was due to appear before the Gacaca hearing.

The Gacaca (meaning "justice on the grass") is a process of local judgment in which the perpetrators of the genocide are brought before the community – in the village or town meeting place – and expected to tell the truth about their involvement. Realizing that using the normal justice system would take at least a hundred years to try the enormous number of cases resulting from the genocide, the Government resorted to a modernized form of the traditional Gacaca system to seek to bring justice. At the Gacaca hearings, survivors who suffered at the hands of the accused, as well as eyewitnesses, are also able to give their account of the events. Everyone is expected to tell the truth about what they have seen or experienced, and they are not allowed to speak about what they have heard second-hand. Anyone summoned to the Gacaca is required to attend – if they are out of the country for any reason, they must return for it.

François' denial of his previous confession was sadly not unusual. A couple of years ago, due to massive prison overcrowding, the Government declared that anyone who confessed their crimes would be freed. Many of the killers confessed, to get out of prison, only to recant their confession once they were released. For the victims of their crimes, this is extremely painful and difficult. It is heartbreaking when the person you know without a shadow of a doubt is guilty of the crime denies it.

It is a two-hour drive from Kigali to Nyanza and then I had to take a motorbike-taxi to the place where the Gacaca was being held. By the time I arrived at the Gacaca it had already started. François was standing in front of all the people who had gathered, holding his hands to his chest. I don't think he had expected to see me ever again and that is why he had lied to me. When I walked in, he turned to look at me and as our eyes met, he immediately looked down. I kept my eyes fixed on him and, seconds later; he looked up again, met my gaze and turned away, swallowing hard. I don't think he had expected me to come all the way from Kigali to the Gacaca and realized that things were not going to go well for him.

I listened as several people came forward to testify that François had been among the killers who had gone to my grandfather's house on May 7, 1994, which he was denying. Addressing François directly, the official presiding over the Gacaca asked, "Did you go in that group, François?"

"No, I did not," he stated.

Then a woman called Donnah rose to her feet. She had been married to my uncle and was one of my mother's close friends. The same band of killers who had murdered my family had murdered her husband and six children. She addressed François directly: "François, you are denying going to Munyabitare's house that morning. If someone who survived your killing spree can testify that you were there, will you still deny it?"

François did not have an answer to her question. He looked down and he appeared to be shaking. Of course, Donnah had been referring to me. I had not come to the Gacaca to try and make François confess that he had been among the group of killers who had murdered my family – I just wanted to hear the truth about my father.

I stood up. First apologizing to the committee and the assembled group of people that I had arrived late, I asked if it was possible for François' statement to be read out again as I had missed it. I felt sure it was going to be different from what he had told me the previous week. Without hesitating, the presiding official read it out again. In it François said he was among the group of killers that had murdered my father. As the statement was being read out François was nervously shuffling from one foot to the other, looking very ashamed. The official asked him whether there was something he wanted to add. At this he said, "I witnessed the death of Bernard and I beat him with a stick, but Karori finished him, and I ask for forgiveness."

I continued: "You see, the last time we spoke, you said you hadn't even approached my dad when he was being killed, but now you are saying that you beat him with a stick. What size was your stick, because I really think that my father was too strong to be killed by a stick?"

"My stick wasn't big. But I didn't kill him, Karori did," he insisted.

Then a woman called Josepha stood up. "You're lying," she said angrily. "We have heard that you killed Bernard after you killed his family. You even took his clothes and his shoes. And I'm sure you were not alone. We can call your fellow killers to come and testify against you. I'm a Hutu like you and I followed all that went on in the genocide. I know you killed Bernard, so don't deny it. Look, you are breaking his daughter's heart – tell the truth so that she can bury her father. Because we all know that it's you who did it." With these words she sat down, looking very annoyed.

After her, a soldier called Innocent got to his feet. He was my father's cousin and the person who had arrested

François after the genocide. He said, "François, what has come over you? Why can't you make things easy for yourself and just tell the truth for once? You yourself told me what happened when I arrested you. You said you'd killed Bernard with a stick after he'd prayed. You told us that he'd given you beer and even that you'd demanded 5000 Rwandan Francs from him, but when you discovered that he only had some dollars and his passport, you refused it, saying you wanted real money not paper, because you didn't even know what dollars were. You told me that you tore the dollars up and threw them on the floor. And now here you are, denying everything."

When Innocent had finished speaking, the presiding official of the Gacaca decided to call to the front a man who had been François's constant companion throughout the genocide. It was Gatoya, my grandfather's killer. Gatoya came forward, looking frightened. His eyes were darting here, there and everywhere as if he was looking for someone, and his hands were clasped tightly together. The presiding official asked him to raise his hand and swear to tell the truth in God's name. When Gatoya had done so, he asked him, "Tell the truth: you were with the group that went to Munyabitare's home and killed people there on the morning of May 7, 1994. Was François with you?"

Without hesitating Gatoya replied, "Yes, he was with us. All we did, we did together. I guess we can't have buried the bodies properly because I hear that Bernard's little girl survived."

"Would you recognize that girl if you saw her?" the presiding official asked.

"No, I don't think so, because it was dark, but I was told in prison that she is alive."

At that moment, I stood up and said, "Gatoya, look at me. I'm the one that you buried alive. Do you know me now?"

"Yes, I know you," he replied.

Then I said, "All I want to know is about my dad, because I know everything else – after all, I was there. Please tell us."

Fear was written all over François's face. He swallowed hard once again and shifted his position. Then the presiding official asked Gatoya, "Can you tell us how many people François killed there?"

"No, I can't tell you how many he killed," Gatoya replied, "because we were all too busy killing. He's the one who can tell you, because he's the one who knows."

The presiding official continued, "Gatoya, can you tell us anything about Bernard's death?"

"Bernard's death? Ask François because he's the one who was responsible for it. I can't say anything because I didn't kill him – François did."

"Thank you," the presiding official said, dismissing Gatoya. "We wanted the truth and now we have it. You can go."

Next to be called was a man called Dismas. Dismas was François's nephew and he had also been among the group that had killed my family. He was a man with a lot of blood on his hands and he had killed many babies. Nevertheless, people used to refer to him as a "man of truth" because he spoke the truth about what had happened and his part in it. When he came forward, people knew they were going to hear what had really happened. Once Dismas was sworn in, the presiding official put his first question: "Dismas, we all know that François is your uncle. Did he go with you to Munyabitare's home the morning his family were killed?"

"Yes, he was with us."

"How many people did you kill there?"

"I really can't say. There were a lot of people there, both old and young. We beat them and then we killed them. I can't say how many," Dismas declared.

"What do you know about Bernard's death?" the presiding official then asked.

"My Uncle François killed him. He knows all the details because he even confessed it in the statement he made."

With the corroborating testimony of these two fellow killers, everyone now knew without a shadow of doubt that François had killed my father. By this time, it was very late and the presiding official of the court concluded the proceedings, saying that the final decision about François's case would be given the following Wednesday. I had to rush off home because it was already dark and I had a long way to go.

As I mulled over the day's events on my journey home, I could feel only pity for François yet I was upset too. I saw how hard it was for him to tell the truth and prayed for him to be released to tell the truth so that he could find peace. Later that evening my family and I prayed together for all the people who had been involved with the Gacaca proceedings that day.

When the Gacaca reassembled the following week, it was without François. He had disappeared, and to this day has not been brought to justice. The decision of the Gacaca, given in his absence, was that François should return to prison because he had not spoken the truth in the statement he had made and was regarded as a danger to society. For me and for many of the families of his other victims, it is very painful to live with the fact that he has neither been brought to justice nor has been forced to divulge the truth about the crimes.

Though I carry no bitterness in my heart towards the killers of my family, it is fundamentally right and proper to see justice carried out on those responsible for heinous acts of bloodshed. Furthermore, the freedom of these killers caused many survivors of the genocide to live in fear. In the rural areas of Rwanda many Tutsi survivors have been murdered to prevent them from testifying against Hutu killers or simply because they testified years ago. It is a very nerve-racking situation. This genocide ideology and genocide denial is still alive and well among the Rwandans. It is also very much known that the last stage of a genocide is always the denial of it.

And so, my search for my father's body continued for many more years. Through later Gacaca trials I have come to hear that François killed my father naked, which put his killing into the highest category of crimes, as it demonstrated that it was a premeditated and deliberate act.

I really thank God that He has enabled me to forgive because now I can live free and move forward with my life. Many people – including many survivors of the genocide – ask me why I choose to forgive my enemies. I tell them that Jesus forgave me, and therefore I must forgive. I wasn't worthy of His forgiveness, but He gave it freely anyway. And people who call themselves followers of Jesus must do the same. I do it for me not just for my enemies. This was the only path to my healing and freedom in God.

Rwanda is a country making good and positive strides forward. A visitor to our beautiful land will see a country whose economy is growing, with flourishing businesses, new houses being built, and a bright, new generation rising full of hope and desiring a better way of life. You do not have to dig very far below the surface, however, to discover that my nation is still hurting very deeply.

In Rwanda when you walk around you see a huge number of young people and young adults. There are many people in their twenties and thirties that grew up as orphans. Many are now married, have children of their own, and are settled in their careers. Because of the genocide women outnumber men by a long way. Thousands of women who were the victims of brutal and repeated rape during the genocide are now suffering from HIV/AIDS. There are many, many survivors of the genocide who have not found a way to come to terms with what happened and are still battling with trauma, loss and pain. A high proportion of these are young people who will carry the trauma they suffered in the formative years of their childhood through the rest of their lives.

After the genocide, there were so many orphans that many people opened their homes to take them in, which was a wonderful thing. But it means that large numbers of these extended families, often headed by a woman on her own, live below the poverty line. Many survivors that were wounded or disabled by the genocide live alone and in poverty with nobody caring for them. There are still so many cases that one cannot close their eyes to.

Each year beginning on April 7 we go through an official week of mourning for the genocide against Tutsis in Rwanda. This memorial period continues for 100 days, which was the exact duration of the genocide. As a result, each year the unhealed, raw wounds are exposed as television and radio programs revisit the events of the genocide. This includes distressing footage of Tutsis being hunted down and killed by Hutus, mutilated and murdered bodies tossed aside in toilets, latrine pits or left by the side of the road, and mass graves containing thousands of corpses. The week is meant to be a memorial; yet during this week, my country is overwhelmed by death once again. This is a good time to teach our younger people the history of our country and to prevent what may bring back the hatred between us. Not just as Rwandans but a lesson to the world too. Churches need to be real about the issues of the genocide, and organizations need to come alongside those who survived but are still suffering. Schools need to teach young children the truth about racism and hatred. Survivors need to speak up and tell their stories of survival and victories. Finally, as a Christian, I believe that prayer is the best gift we can give to our nations. For I know what my nation has been through and I couldn't bear for another generation to have to face the hatred we had to face. Prayer and faith in action changes all things.

Chapter 12
Finding My Father's Body Remains

After my first book *Frida, Chosen to Die, Destined to Live* was published I did many book tours and book signings in England, Germany, and many other places. People asked questions about finding my father's body. Sometimes I had no answers; other times my answer was short with a big sigh: "I am still searching". A lot of survivors in the country have been able to give a decent burial to their loved ones, just like my mum, my grandparents and my siblings were given a decent burial while I was in Gabon. I missed out on this important part of my life and that caused me to always wonder if I would ever be able to find my father's body remains so I can find closure. I had attended Gacaca courts several times and visited prisons trying to find the whole truth from people who killed my family, since Francois had disappeared, but they were not truthful. I never stopped looking.

In 2007 I had two little children; my biological son Maxwell was 3, my beautiful little girl Natasha that I had adopted as a baby was then 2 years old, and I was pregnant with my third. Even though I was heavily pregnant I kept going back and forth asking people in the village.

During a disturbing phone call from my uncle in November 2007, I learnt that my father's body had been found – but that the head was missing. The call came while I was in a hair salon a week after giving birth to Asher-Regis, whom I had named after my youngest brother. There is an expression in the Kinyarwanda language that refers to someone's "lost or missing head." Because of the many thoughts and mixed feelings going through my mind, I misunderstood my uncle's message. I thought he said that they had found my father alive, but that he had gone insane. "No, Frida", he said. "We found his body, but his head (skull) is missing."

I got up from the hood dryer, with all kinds of emotions, and I asked him: "How do you know it's him and where did you find him?" He replied: "We found his body remains in a swamp not too far away from your home. We've got his identification card, driver's license and a few other items from his pockets. You can still read his name, Frida. That is how we know it is him." I couldn't contain myself. I started crying. One part of me was so sad and heartbroken. Another part was relieved and happy that I had finally gotten closure, and that my prayers had been answered. I went home right away. My cousin Clarisse was with me. We had gone to the salon together. She started calling some of our family members. One of the special people in my life, my mum's brother Aime, promised that he would come to my house early next morning to accompany me to the scene.

I was up all night, crying. At that time, I had been married for four years but my marriage was in a terrible state due to the abusive behaviors and multiple affairs of the man

I had married. I had kept this a secret, so not many people knew what I was going through. We were leading a growing church but my life was miserable. I covered it all with a smile. We had three little children: a three and half year old, Maxwell; a two and a half year old, Natasha; and a one week baby Asher, along with a few other teenagers we had taken in. Early the next morning, my mum's brother and his cousin came to my house and I was ready to go. I left the children at home with my maid. We drove to Nyanza. As soon as we got to my grandfather's house, I was taken to the room where my father's remains were. I couldn't believe what my eyes were seeing. A man everyone respected was reduced to almost nothing. I recognized his handkerchief. It was in a square shape still well pressed and ironed, exactly the way my mum had taught me. She had given this to my papa right before the genocide. I saw his identity card and driver's license, but the fact that I couldn't find his skull, was enough reason not to bury him. I felt like an important part was still missing.

So now I knew that what I had heard at the Gacaca court years before about my father being killed naked was not even true. Survivors simply recognized their loved ones by the clothing they were wearing when they were killed. My father's cousin and his son had also discovered my father's identity card and driver's license. You could still see his picture and read his names, as well as the tribe name Tutsi that was always indicated right below the picture.

After looking at his remains and wiping off my tears, I took another deep breath and went away to pray to ask the Lord to give me the courage to face this all one more time. This time with a much more burdened heart, I had no idea how to approach all of this and how I would react when I met those who had treated my dad's body this cheaply. It was clear that whoever did this did not care for me either. Survivors were being killed from time to time because of the testimonies they had given in Gacaca court. The country was facing another phase of genocide as ex-prisoners and their people, still holding to their genocide ideologies and anger, kill survivors in order to wipe out the truth.

As soon as I finished praying I decided to go see one man to whom I had mentioned that I would never stop looking for my father's body. I had told the man that I would keep coming to him until he told me where my father's body remains were. This was a man whom I had mentioned at the Gacaca court. At the court, I had explained that I had heard this man's voice yelling that my father had just been killed. Yet this man denied it and said that he was not even in the area when my dad was killed. He had said that he was shopping in Gatagara that day and that he only learnt about my father's death when he returned that night. Nobody believed what I was saying, but I was convinced that this man knew about my father's death. His name is Kanambiye and he was one of those who convinced the Gacaca court that all the people being accused were innocent. As a result,

Kanambiye never went to jail. All those years that I was searching he tried to discourage me. The last time he had seen me I was pregnant with my youngest baby. I told the man that I would always keep searching for my father's remains until the day I got old and died. If my efforts were unsuccessful, the baby that I was expecting would take on the responsibilities to keep searching.

So I got up and asked my cousin Erickson to accompany me to Kanambiye's house. Somehow my heart was telling me that Kanambiye might be the one who had done this. My father's remains had been moved from where he was killed and dumped in the ditch close to my home, which I was trying to rebuild at the time. Erickson had been in the army so I was confident that he would protect me in case anything happened. In addition, I was no longer scared anymore but angry. Kanambiye ran away when he and others saw us walking up the hill to his home from my grandfather's house. His wife and son were home, however, and lied to us when we got there. I told her that I was willing to make peace with them if they told me the truth. Otherwise, it would not be good.

She said she had no idea where her husband had gone. I told her that I had seen more than two people as we were walking down the hill, and that her husband couldn't be too far away. I explained that she needed to find him immediately or else I would involve the police right away. Upon hearing that, she went and told him to come from wherever he had been hiding. When he arrived, I asked him to give me my father's head. I did not want to give him a second to think twice or to show that I doubted the fact that I knew he had done this. He said he had no idea what I was talking about and that he had nothing to do with my father s death. I reminded him of what I had said to him a few months earlier – that I would not stop looking until I find out where my father's body remainders was – and that if I passed before then my son would take on the task. He remembered those words. I then said, "Well that day is this." "I found him but I need him in full – not parts missing".

The more he denied it the more his face, eyes and body language betrayed him. After so many hours of trying to solve this ourselves, we decided to involve the police. Close to my old home was a newly built prison, which meant it was the closest place where we could find soldiers or police to help us. When the leader of that prison – who was also a Major in the Army – appeared at my grandfather's home, he told us that the news of what happened to me and my family had traveled to him very quickly. We explained to him what we were facing and how long we had been trying to ask Kanambiye if he knew anything about my father's body and its missing head. The prison leader said that Kanimbiye would help us on the condition that I would have to help find and dig it up. And we all wondered why?

When the Major who led the prison talked with Kanambiye, his story changed again. This time he said, "I may try and help but I have no idea what these people are accusing me of." While being questioned at the scene, Kanambiye admitted that he had dug my father's remains out and threw them in that ditch because I had kept going back to him ask for them. It was already late in the evening and I knew I had left my babies all day so I needed to get back home. The Major also said that since he knew a little bit of the truth, he would take Kanambiye to jail so he could confess it all.

That night traveling back to Kigali, my heart was aching so bad because of this whole scenario that had brought a lot of bad memories back to me. And seeing all that had happened to my father was just so cruel. I also went back into the days when I had told the Gacaca Court people that Kanambiye knew everything about my father's death and no one believed me, this hurt me too.

The following day my cousin Erickson called me to tell me that Kanambiye had confessed everything. He told the Major all about the other two men and Kanambiye's son – who was only 14 – who helped him pull my father's remains and throw them in that ditch. In addition, after his confessing and after they brought these other two guys and Kanambiye's son they all told the truth of where they had put my father's skull.

Out of curiosity, the Major asked them again why they would do such a thing. Kanambiye said that it was so I would keep hurting having not found my father's remains.

When they told me that, I concluded that if I had ever gone to this guy alone he could have even killed me if he hated me this much. Also, my heart could not believe that after forgiving these people who hurt us so much they still had so much hatred towards survivors. We all know that they do not love us and that if some of them were given a chance, they would do it again as some of them even say, but I had no idea it was this bad.

When Erickson told me the whole story over the phone, I could not control my tears, yet thanking God for revealing all this truth using my cousin, the Prison Leader and all those kids who had seen my father's body in that ditch. Later we went back to that same ditch and picked other pieces of my father's remains and we reburied him on December 8, 2007. This was like the end of my journey. My two little kids were there, all my friends who could make it supported me, and my mom and dad's friends were there. I felt like my father was honored as he really deserved it. The words I spoke on that day were not words of anger, but deep sorrow and deep sense of rest for me. I was so thankful to God who had given me a chance to come to terms with my whole family gone and put to rest all together. The one thing that has helped me hold it together so often is to ask the Lord for his grace at every stage of my life. So I did on this day also. God's grace carried me through that day. As for Kanambiye, though, I will not lie: I did not want to see that man's face or his wife's.

Later on, his wife brought me a letter he wrote while in prison. The letter said that he was very sorry and that he knew me as a forgiving person and that maybe I should ask God to give me grace to forgive him too just like me had forgiven others. I felt these were words of manipulation and that he wanted me to feel guilty if I did not forgive him as a Christian. But forgiveness should never be from words of manipulation; nor should it be imposed on anyone. Forgiveness should be an act of faith and willingness from the victim. Also, forgiveness does not mean trust. Just because we forgave someone does not mean we will trust that person. If I had forgiven Kanambiye and let him return to the community (authority I did not have anyway), he would be a danger to those around him, especially to other survivors who lived in my village. I still wanted him to face justice. I'm not the only survivor in the area who could have suffered from his evil plans. I have extended family that are related to my father, and asking the police to release Kanambiye would have been the worst thing I could ever do to my father's brother or his cousins who were still angry about Kanambiye's choices.

All this happened while I was rebuilding my family home that had been demolished during the genocide. But I did not let it discourage me from finishing the home I loved. All I wanted was to find healing through rebuilding the home where I experienced a happy childhood and the joy of having a family. Also, it was during this time that my extended family member Manzi, who was the main builder, a wonderful young man and only survivor of his family, was killed. The evening he came to meet me and get the money to buy all the materials we needed was the evening he was robbed and shot dead. What a trying and hard time for his wife and four little kids he left behind. It was heartbreaking to lose such a man that we all knew as a man of integrity and love for all people.

Manzi was also the man that was helping all of us as survivors in my village to prepare and get our memorial site ready for the commemoration that year, and he was killed a week before we had it. The following year, Manzi's widow lost one of her children too through a hit and run. How much could someone like her, who was also the only survivor of her family, suffer within a short period of time? A lot happened at this time that could have stopped me from accomplishing the goal of rebuilding my home, but I had made up my mind that no matter what happened, those who had killed my family and were still targeting my family members would not see me fail.

I later had a chance to hire other builders, and thanks to God a few months afterwards my home was completed. It was a sign of restoration in some sense. Some people asked me, "Why are you wasting your money if you know you are not even going to live there?" My desire was to bring back my family honor and avoid losing the land because the laws were changing in Rwanda and if I was not using or developing such a big land it would have been possible for the government to give it away to someone else who was capable of developing it. That would have meant not only losing my family, but also my family legacy and those wonderful memories I had there. I knew my Mama and Papa would have done the same if they had survived. Rebuilding this home gave me a greater sense of hope. It is amazing how a small act such as rebuilding or picking up the pieces can mean so much to a survivor.

Later on I took my children every other weekend so they could enjoy what I enjoyed as a kid. Running around without worrying about cars around, jumping and yelling without minding about the neighbors next door as it was a big field of land. Still, one important element was missing: the love I had felt there as a child. No grandparents, no family, just graves and the sense of fear that overwhelmed me from time to time of what may happen to my little kids and me while we were there. I could not stay later than 6:00 pm as it started to get dark, and I did not trust all those men who had been released from prison and who knew I came there very often. I could also not bear the feeling of spending the night in that house without my family there.

My family later enjoyed all kinds of vegetables I planted with the help of a family I let live in the home, and milk from our own cows and so on. The joy I felt during all these activities brought much. The pride and the confidence of knowing that I had rebuilt something very important and part of me was felt every time I travelled there with family and friends. My hope was that this time my children's children would get to see that home. It was also good for my children to see that no matter what the enemy intended to destroy in my life I did not allow myself to be defeated and I had kept the legacy of my family. Looking at my little kids playing, running up and down the hill outside my home, warmed my heart and put a smile on my face at the same time wishing mama would see what kind of a mother I had become.

    I made sure I bought every animal that we had as I was growing up: cows, goats, sheep, turkey, hens, dogs, cats, you name it. My kids loved them, especially Asher my youngest who loves animals, just like my dad and youngest brother Regis. Surely this was a sign of a new beginning. I still missed my mum's smile, my brothers and sister's laughter and the presence of my father. Some neighbors still came whenever we visited, and it felt exactly like when my dad came home for the weekend. This reminded me of how I used to see people in front of our door, venting to my dad and asking for help. It's hard to think that after all the help my father had given people in that community, they had taken his life themselves. The amazing part of all was to see my children play with those former neighbors' grand kids. My kids had no hatred and neither did the neighbors' from what I saw. This showed me how hatred is a learnt behavior; it is like a seed planted in people's minds and injected into our lives either by our own parents or leaders. Maybe the neighbors' kids had no idea yet of what their parents had done or they were too little to even wonder what had happened to the neighbors they never met.

My own kids were too little to understand what had happened to my family then; however, they knew that the grandparents and uncles on my side had been killed. That was all they knew at their age.

A legacy of godliness, kindness and grace is supposed to be passed on by a parent. Not a gift of anger and bitter roots. That is how we can rebuild and restore what has been damaged in us. Not repaying evil with evil.

Chapter 13
A Lesson of Faith and Resilience

The year 2011 was another trying time, as I went through separation and then divorce. I could not believe that I was going through another painful period and sense of loss. It surely felt again like a time of grief, this time as a mother with three young children. In the middle of this crisis I moved to the USA. In this process I also lost most of my friends who did not feel that it was right to divorce and said that since I was able to forgive those who had killed my family I should also forgive the father of my children. What they had forgotten though or did not understand was that I had forgiven and forgiven again but could not trust any more.

The more stories I discoveredabout my ex-husband's affairs, the more I was broken until I decided not to want to listen any more. I understood that I would not know the whole truth, and I was not sure I needed to know the whole truth anymore. I was deceived and abused, and my whole world had fallen apart again.

In a new culture, without many friends or family, I decided to go back to school and finish my college degree.

With the support of a group of loving believers who welcomed me to Norwalk, Ohio, and allowed God to use them I was able to graduate with a Bachelor's degree in Communication. Going full time for four years nonstop and working and raising three kids did not make it easy at all, but

I was determined. Sometimes I only slept for one to three hours, which often affected my emotions. When you are depressed, concentrating is a task itself, so I sometimes had to read a page of my homework twice or three times to make sense of what I was reading. I was also translating some of what I was reading into French or Kinyarwanda to understand it better and then translate it back into English. I was put on antidepressants, something I and my culture were so against. I was certain that I was going to depend on them for the rest of my life, but I never stopped crying to God to heal my broken heart. I remember once owning a necklace with a broken heart medal and my Doctor, who is a Christian, saw it during my appointment and said to me, "I see that you are wearing a broken heart, is that how you feel?" I replied that I did not mean to wear my heart on my sleeves, but I guess I was too broken to even realize that it was showing in what I chose to wear. I thank God that he later delivered me from those pills and healed my depression.

    I cannot tell you how hard this was and how many times I would burst into tears in the middle of a lesson. I would excuse myself and cry uncontrollably in the school bathrooms or in my car driving home so my children could not see my tears. Once I got home after school, though, I would put on a happy mom face to my children and drive to all those evening activities like many moms in the USA. I attended counseling from time to time as I realized I was falling apart. The pain was much deeper this time: it was inflicted by the one person I had chosen out of many that said they liked me and wanted to marry me. I had offered my whole life to this man. I had trusted a man who said he loved me yet did not consider me enough for him. I always wondered if I was not pretty enough or was too much for him to handle. It also hurt so much because he had seen me heal before and he knew all I had been through before I met him yet he still betrayed me and our kids.

    My counselor and his wife always said to me that I must know that it had nothing to do with what I was or wasn't, did or did not do and that it was his responsibility to assume. It was easy to hear, but it took a long time to sink into my heart. I felt like a liar and I was ashamed because I had protected this man for years and covered all he had done to me and to others with a smile on my face and confessed that all was well with us as I had always dreamed. I was so angry not only at him but at myself for being so fooled while some of my family members had warned me before marrying him. I felt like I could not tell my story of forgiveness any more as I was struggling to forgive the person I had had kids with and had loved. All I wanted was to hide and disappear, but my sponsor and the family that had welcomed me to America as their own always encouraged me to keep moving forward and to not stop my speaking. They would say, "few years from now things will be different." But to be honest it was so hard for me to see how my life could heal from this pain.

In the eyes of my people back home my fears were realized. Divorce is unheard of, especially if you are a pastor's wife. You are to forgive and remain, even if the other person does not change their behavior. It is true we do not have to wait for a person to change before we can forgive, however remaining in a situation of ongoing unfaithfulness and abuse is a different matter altogether.

I would receive emails and texts from people in Rwanda, including those from my former church, calling me evil for divorcing, or telling me that I needed to get back with my ex-husband, as simple as that. At this time all I needed was prayer and grace but I got judgment. A friend of mine who went through the same thing recently told me, "Do not be surprised when people start judging you before they can listen to you, it's how it goes." She was right: as to divorce I had no idea how painful it was until I endured it. This ordeal opened my eyes and taught me not to judge others before I hear their side of the story.

In the middle of that depression, I made sure I surrounded myself with prayers, asking a few friends to pray when I could not pray for myself and my kids. In faith, I knew I could not give up. Again it was not a time to give up as I was now living my life for three others - my children. I also wanted them to see and learn that you can still accomplish your goals no matter how many obstacles get in your way. It is in the midst of this pain that I learnt how to stand and walk by faith. I learnt to live by what I knew was true versus what I felt (2 Corinthians 5:8). For we walk by faith not by sight. I can assure you that if you were to walk and act by how you feel every day, you would miss so many days at work and probably lose your job. Or if all you did was not talk to people every time you felt like not talking, you would end up losing all your friends and probably more. This does not mean that we can't talk about our feelings or can't be truthful about how we feel. Trust me, I'm the kind of person that expresses her feelings easily and speaks her mind, but I do not always trust or walk according to my feelings. I sometimes question my own feelings before I act on them or make a decision based on them. Because I have learnt that feelings are fickle and change from time to time, especially for a person like me who was so broken. You always want to be careful not to make decisions based on how you feel but on the truth and facts. Then grow even on the level of acting according to the word of God.

    In this process I learnt to be real with my own feelings instead of pushing them down or masking them with a smile. I voiced them when needed, I said if I was tired, I cried when I felt like crying and I screamed in my car when driving alone. I sometimes felt like I was losing my mind but I knew when to stop and pray or when to call someone that was close to me and tell them how terrible I felt. It was such a trying and hard time for me, yet I knew that God's grace covered me and his mercy followed me each new day. I also knew that the greatest help I needed was from above, so I called on the name of Jesus every time I felt like I was sinking. I needed his grace and mercies to help me each day, so I cried unto God for that to help me through my problems. I once heard someone say that even though God's grace is new every morning, you do not need the grace of a widow if you are not one. You do not need the grace of an orphan if you are not one, but as soon as something like this happens to you there is that grace that will carry you through it. I now believe this to be true. When a situation comes into our lives God is always ready to send the appropriate grace for that very situation, and it is up to you to accept it or waste it. Prior to becoming a single mom you couldn't imagine how you would survive, but when faced with it, you receive that specific grace. He is a faithful God and all powerful in each situation. All you need is to ask for that grace, and trust that he will send it.

Maxwell was growing now to ask a lot of questions about my family, as did my other two children. I could not say much about the brutal killing or tell them details of how my family was killed because I have to be careful that I do not tell them my story in a way that will build anger and hatred. But I was also not going to lie to them. They knew I spoke at a lot of places and schools around where we live and so I explained to them what happened with words they could understand. To this day I get questions from them especially from Asher Regis, the youngest, who has so much in common with his namesake, my youngest brother Regis. In fact, we used to call Asher by what is now his middle name, Regis. At the age of three however, he fell sick and it scared me and made me think he could even die like my brother. So I switched his names and told my family to call him Asher (which was his middle name back then). I did not want to lose another Regis. Fortunately he is a healthy boy now and growing so fast.

    People ask me how I did it, raising three kids on my own, going to college full-time, working and still live my life. I tell them that I tried to quit so many times, but then after I talked to my family members or a good friend about quitting, I would rethink my decision and choose to try again, believing in the Lord, praying and pushing myself. The Lord did it all; he fought all my battles. At times I felt like I had no strength to move, and that I was the person that lost everything, but I also knew that if I only kept looking at what I lost and feeling sorry for myself, it was only going to increase my depression.

    I woke up every morning at 5 am, had my devotion, laid hands on each of my children in their beds and got ready for the day. After talking about our day, we would also sing our Kinyarwanda songs, dance and pray for each other's needs before bed. Whatever we prayed and waited for as a family, we saw happen, and this has been a great testimony to my kids to this day. I remember after my niece Mimi graduation from college, we prayed every night that she would get a job, and she did. Maxwell could not make friends and was struggling at school because of that and we prayed for a good friend for him. Not long after, he got a really good friend that was nice to him. This may sound trivial, but they are huge in the eyes of my kids. It was an opportunity for me to teach them that prayer and trust in God can change the way we see our situation.

I never knew how hard it was for a single mom to raise kids alone, even when in my case I had support from different people that the Lord sent my way. I'm sure there are so many single women or men who feel like they are drowning, have so few resources or no time to even rest. Through this experience I developed great compassion for those women who are abused and who feel the pain of betrayal, feel beaten down and left alone to raise their children. I also learnt that the key to strength is not to hide from your struggles, but to scream out loud to God and get some help from friends or professionals.

Refusing to fail in your heart is half the answer to finding the courage for moving on. Positive thinking and confessing that you can carry on all endeavors through Christ who strengthens you is another weapon in life that you need when you are going through loss. It is very easy to become negative in this negative and in difficult situations, but trying hard and training yourself to see and fix your eyes on the positive, even if it is just one blessing you see in your life, is important. I would rather confess one positive blessing in my life all day, than count and recount all the wrongs that happened.

I kept speaking and telling my story even when I did not feel like it or when I felt I did not want anyone to listen to me anymore. Through my speaking engagements I was giving to others, which helped me a lot. The best thing you can ever do for yourself when you are depressed is to do something nice for someone else.

You do not give because you have a lot; you give because you have discovered the secret of life. Life is all about giving and receiving and it is a greater blessing to give than to receive. We cannot only take and simply survive. Just look at a very simple example from life related to breathing. You take a breath in, but cannot survive without a breath out. When you are a victim or survivor of a horrific event like genocide, it is easy to want people to listen to you and help you, which is great, but if you are not returning that blessing to anyone it can be dangerous. You can inadvertently grow a sense of self-pity and selfishness. In order to break these habits, you need to learn to teach yourself to give to others that have been in the same situation, or to your community, your church, or even those you do not know.

I have spoken worldwide and my story has been shared with people I'm not sure I will ever meet. I have received encouraging comments as well as very cruel ones, but that has never stopped me from telling the world about what happened to my people. I have so much to share with the younger generation and the generations to come. For me, speaking is a way of giving to others and serving by being a voice for my loved ones that were killed and will never be heard again and also those who are traumatized and cannot speak for themselves.

We have so many unheard stories of mothers who lost their children and husbands with so much pain. We have young survivors in their twenties that were very young when the genocide happened and who are unable to recall what happened. This is why I encourage my fellow survivors to speak up about their loss and broken hearts and by so doing, perhaps save another life somewhere in the world. Racism is not a root that has died completely. It is still alive and well and we see it in the world.

If you ask me why I choose to share, my reply is that not only have I received healing through my speaking, but the work of speaking also encourages others and helps them understand that no matter what we go through, we can still bounce back and be useful in our communities, churches, and in the world. I have learnt that through speaking publically, you may actually save lives. People suffer so much in different parts of the world, and by speaking about our experience of healing, someone else who is planning on taking their own life may be encouraged to get help and be saved.

The simple act of cleaning a sick person's house,

helping a disabled survivor wounded by the genocide, listening to someone's story, or even using your pain to help someone who is at the place of wanting or thinking of committing suicide, can make such a difference. Giving is an act of healing. I have also found that as a mother, giving, and serving my children has healed so many areas of my wounded life. I sometimes wonder what life would be without my three angels and what joy would be missing in my life. Even though I get so tired taking care of all the three of them, I find so much joy seeing them grow each day, especially seeing how much they love the Lord and enjoy being part of our church activities. I always pray that I grow old seeing my grandkids do the same.

Chapter 14
Healing Through Relationships

As survivors, one very important aspect of life we lost was relationships with those we loved with all our hearts. We lost mothers who loved and nurtured us; we lost fathers who provided and protected us; we lost siblings who were a source of meaning of what life is all about, and grandparents who were the source of wisdom and guidance to us. We lost friends who gave us a sense of joy.

When you lose so much in such short period of time it is easy to isolate yourself from all relationships or build a wall around yourself to keep everyone else outside your world. Isolation however, is a prison that can damage you even more. This is a dangerous place where you believe your own self-talk and your own perspectives, and you become your own mentor or own hero, which is wrong. Time alone is needed sometimes but time to feel lonely can become a self-pity party that no one else around you wants to join. A self-pity party, wherein we say we want to be alone, is often a cry for help. Sometimes people around you care enough to get the message; other times they really don't even want to get involved with that kind of person fearing they may be hurt themselves or that it is too much work for them. But there is always the unchanging friend in Christ, who is not scared of any situation, not even our rejection of him. He still waits even when we get to the point of shutting him out, like I did when my family was taken away and I was angry at God for not protecting us.

A friend of mine once told me that when she was going through a divorce, she felt like people were running away from her. Some of her friends did not want to get closer to her as she kept it real and said the way she felt each time someone asked, and she ended up noticing some of her friends turning away when they saw her. Some people even in churches want to only be around people who are talking and thinking positive. Some preachers even teach this, "be around those people who can build you up, not those who speak negatively and bring you down." But how about what Jesus said, "mourn with those who mourn"?

Yes it is true when people are caught up in self-pity, they are hard to deal with but no one said that being a Christian or a committed friend was an easy job. Once we commit ourselves to each other as friends or even marriage relationships it means the person will not always have good days. Being Christians or friends means going to those who need us and those who cannot carry their own burdens sometimes no matter what the season. When we turn our backs on them, even when they are seemingly rejecting us, we are not being a good example and cannot expect them to do the same for someone else when they get out of that pit of depression.

When I was sixteen years old, and because of my traumas, I started believing my own lies that nobody loved me, that I was useless, a burden to my extended family, and not a good friend to anyone. I started locking myself in the school bathroom, which smelled so bad we called them a mine field (or bomb). As teenagers who had just lived through war and genocide, the worst thing we could compare our bathroom smell to was a bomb (meaning too much to bear). I would lock myself in there and cry nonstop refusing to talk to my best friends about how I felt. I would then tell myself that I should kill myself instead of being a burden to everyone. Even though I would lock myself in there alone, deep down I wished someone heard me and asked me what was wrong. Yet when my friends did, I would not say anything. But my three friends Fille, Karabo my cousin and Dylove, who were also my roommates, would not give up on me. Especially Fille. Whenever she did not see me in the evening laughing with the group then she knew where to find me and would cry at the bathroom door begging me to come out so we could talk.

My thoughts became actions, and I attempted to kill myself with an overdose of pills during that semester. This failed as I was quickly taken to hospital when my friends found me. A few weeks later, with so much shame, I was well again and came back to the same school. I was the talk of the school and while giving a speech, the principal even referred to my suicide attempt, which made my situation even worse. I felt like everyone thought of me as crazy now and that I was going to lose all my friends and would never be taken seriously because I would be referred to as that girl who tried to commit suicide. I sometimes overheard guys talk behind my back as I passed by, saying something like "she is pretty, but crazy to try to commit suicide. What is the matter with her?" and this was another shame I was going to carry the rest of life.

This is one example of how I had locked everyone else out and had decided I was my own friend, yet not even a good friend to myself. But it is also a good example of how my friends never gave up on me even when I pushed them away. It was not until I allowed the Lord into my life and decided to trust and believe in him again that faith opened doors for me to let others in my life too. It all started with rebuilding and accepting the most important and wonderful relationship with Christ the giver of life. I related to him in prayer, worship and even speaking to him like I was speaking to a friend I knew very well. When situations went bad I went on my knees and cried to him like I would to my own father or mother.

At times I could not express how I felt and was overwhelmed and would let tears be my prayer believing that he understood what I meant and where I was coming from. I felt safe in his arms pouring out my heart. Sometimes I would even cry myself to sleep, but I did not walk back as I knew that he accepted me no matter what. I also knew that there was no emotion of mine that could scare him. My situation was no bigger than what Job from the Bible endured, and since that did not scare God, neither should mine. At least I had no wounds over my body like him, and my friends had not left me nor my extended family as in that case of Job's wife. No one was asking me to curse God and die, so my situation was no closer to where Job was when God rescued him. I then started by making friends in church, joined the youth choir, later even started and led a youth group in my high school of APE Rugunga. I also started a small choir for younger girls 10 - 12 years and they loved me so much just as much as I loved them.

    Today, I hear from many of them that live in different parts of the world still telling me how my leadership helped them get to where they are today. One girl that was part of this young girls' choir is now married and has three children and lives in Maine in the USA. She and her husband have a ministry that preaches the word of God and posts messages on YouTube. Recently she wrote to me and said, "It has taken me a long time to say this to you, but I never forgot that one day I should tell you that I'm who I am today because of you. You impacted my life with the way you led that group and made me realize how serious life was and that following Christ was the only option. And now I'm in ministry and seeing you finish school with three children on your own shows me what a strong woman you are." Allowing people in our lives and giving to others helps us move forward.

I allowed my family to love me and decided to smile to each person I met. I decided I was beautiful, and that people loved me and that people wanted to be with me and around me. I would literally speak to myself in a mirror that I was very pretty and valuable and this built confidence in me. It was through allowing friends to love and help me that I learnt helping others. It is through speaking to people and building friendships that I'm even in America today raising my children and having graduated with a Bachelor's degree. If I had not met the family that sponsored me and allowed them to love me as I loved them back I would not have been able to come to Bowling Green State University Firelands Campus and finish college. Maybe I wouldn't even have the job I have now or be with the church that I go to. I have learnt that when you listen to the people that have your best interest at heart, you are gaining more respect and friendship, which will heal your heart. People hate people, but people can also love people. There are bad people in the world yes, but there are still great people in the world also. Not allowing what happened to you be the cause of hurting yourself and others by isolating yourself, is the beginning of a great journey of healing. Then allowing people to love you, and returning the love, is even a greater blessing that will bring more healing.

Relationships heal a broken heart and no man is an island as they say. No matter how much I lost in life, I have also learnt that family is where they love me and that family is where they receive me. It is for that reason I have so many people that I call sisters and brothers in the world that are not related to me biologically at all. It is true that when we are hurt, we may isolate ourselves as our wounds are still fresh, but it is important to be willing and to desire that healing. Asking for help when it is needed is not a weakness; instead, it is courage. The relationships we form or build with people around us and with God are very important parts of the journey of healing. I have experienced this kind of healing by letting the right people in my life.